WHERE HEAVEN AND

BOOKS BY DANNY SIEGEL

*Out of Print

(COMBINED EDITION)

WHERE HEAVEN AND EARTH TOUCH

תא אחוי לך היכא דנשקא ארעא ורקיעא אהדדי

(Baba Batra 74a)

Midrash and Halachah

Compiled and Translated by

DANNY SIEGEL

with a
Topical Index by Beth Huppin

THE TOWN HOUSE PRESS

Pittsboro, North Carolina

I am grateful to the Jewish Publication Society of America for giving me permission to use translations and adaptations of translations from their editions of *The Torah* (1962), *The Prophets* (1978), and *The Writings* (1982).

First Printing as a Combined Volume 1996
Second Printing 1992
Third Printing 1996

Library of Congress Catalog Number: 83-50225.
International Standard Book Number: 0-9406-53-09-5

Printed in the United States of America.

Cover Illustration by Fran Schultzberg.

CONTENTS

BOOK ONE

TABLE OF CONTENTS: Book One

INTRODUCTION

"Passionate, Gutsy Torah" would have been an appropriate additional subtitle for this pamphlet, or "Torah and Life-Values." These passages taken from the Talmud, Midrash, Law Codes, and other traditional volumes—including many off-the-beaten-track texts—have been anthologized for one purpose: exploring the relationship between Torah and the search for Menschlichkeit, human being, decency, caring, a benevolent reaching out. My hope is that people will be intellectually stimulated, but even more so, to be moved, touched, given pause to consider what Judaism has to say about how we live our lives as Jews. Insight and lyric are the topics more than plain acquisition of facts.

Wisdom is the subject. Menschlichkeit, a goal always only partially attainable, is the essence of Torah-study as I see it, an immense struggle, worthwhile despite the immensity. Surrounded as we are by paganism, cynicism, arrogance, and a culture that breeds egocentricity, this is a modest attempt to redirect our vision. Ignorance destroys—that is a truism. But there is also a kind of destructive knowledge, and I would wish by the easy availability of the pamphlet to bring to light a different view of knowledge, one that points to actions that allow us to rise above ourselves and the insufficient values swirling around us every day.

This is a pamphlet for adults, though it may be used as a text in Hebrew highschools, too. The Talmud, Maimonides, and Shulchan Aruch all incontrovertibly rule that adult education is more important than education of the children. Selection #1 says exactly that. I believe it is a source of great detriment to the welfare of our communities that we have not taken this insight to heart. Rarely do adult education courses center on the topics of Menschlichkeit, Edelkeit—Jewish nobility of soul, Ehrlichkeit—honesty and uprightness, Ziesskeit—human sweetness, and Shaynkeit—the inner beauty of the individual soul. It is hoped that this pamphlet will be used for courses and minicourses, in synagogues and Chavurot and small home study groups, in one-on-one *chavruta*-exchanges, and by individuals. We are in great need of the "Redignification of Adult Jewish Study," and this is perhaps a small first step.

The pamphlet is also intended as a leaf-through book. Allowing the eye and mind to fall randomly on some selection, to consider a change of vision, an adjustment of our actions—this, too, would be worthwhile—as well as more formalized study settings.

I am not a scholar, but rather a student of Torah and a poet. Nearly twenty years ago I purchased a copy of Professor Nahum N. Glatzer's *Hammer On The Rock, A Midrash Reader*. . . . texts without commentary. My copy is well-worn from re-reading and teaching and re-teaching the material. As I read or leafed through the slender book, modest doors and brilliantly shining gates both opened to me, views of worlds I did not suspect existed in Jewish life. I would allow my mind to roll and bend and turn and wander, and wonder at the profundities and suggestibilities of the texts presented to me. Over the years, the texts changed meanings, re-arranged themselves into different priorities and possibilities, moving me in different ways. I would hope that this volume, too, will do the same for others to some degree, though I do not pretend to have at my disposal the vast storehouse of Torah knowledge and wisdom that Professor Glatzer has.

As a student of Torah, I have remained essentially faithful to the text, translating as carefully as my abilities allowed, but also freeing myself from literalistic tendencies when I felt the lyricism of the words demanded a more intuitive, singing rendition. I began my writing career as a poet, and see now that with certain passages I needed to be free, grasping for the spirit of the words as well as the exact sense. I have also knowingly taken many selections out of context. While scholars may view this with an element of disfavor, I believe, nevertheless, that the pedagogical goal justifies this approach.

The selections are varied and out of balance—too much here, too little there. *Where Heaven and Earth Touch* is a rather personal selection, though, intended to whet the appetite, to offer the student and casual peruser an opportunity to go beyond this selection—to the *Encyclopaedia Judaica, Hammer on the Rock*, Klagsbrun's excellent *Voices of Wisdom*, Montefiore and Loewe's *A Rabbinic Anthology*, Ginzberg's work of genius *The Legends of the Jews*, other anthologies, and, of course, the sources in the original. While it is hoped that all Jews will enjoy the unique pleasure of opening the giant volumes of Talmud, Midrash, and Law Codes in the Hebrew and Aramaic, for now, English translations will have to serve as an intermediate step. No one should be robbed of the privilege of passionate Torah study.

As I have been allowed into the world of Torah values and the glorious struggle to interact with those values, so, too, may you, with the moderate assistance of this volume, enjoy the wonders of Torah.

Danny Siegel
March 7, 1983

TORAH

1. If a parent wished to study Torah, and he has a child who must also learn—the parent takes precedence. However, if the child is more insightful or quicker to grasp what there is to be learned, the child takes precedence. Even though the child gains priority thereby, the parent must not ignore his own study, for just as it is a Mitzvah to educate the child, so, too, is the parent commanded to teach himself.

Maimonides, Mishna Torah,
Laws of Torah Study 1:4

2. Rav Ya'acov the son of Rav Acha bar Ya'acov was sent by his father to study with Abayye.

When his father came to observe, he saw that his son was not learning well.

He said, "I can do better than you. Return home, and I will take your place."

Kiddushin 29b

3. Who is truly wise?

One who learns from all people.

Pirke Avot 4:1

One who foresees the consequences of his acts.

Tamid 32a

One who lives out what he has learned.

Sifray, Deuteronomy 1, Piska 13

4. Rabbah the son of Rav Huna said:

Whoever possesses Torah-knowledge but has no fear of sin is like a treasurer who has been given the keys to the inner doors, but not to the outer doors. How could he possibly get in to reach the treasure?

Shabbat 31a–b

5. When a teacher is teaching, and the students do not understand, he should not be angry at them or become upset, but rather he should go over the material again and again—even many times—until they understand the depth of the law. Similarly, a student should not say, "I understand," if he has not understood. He should ask again—many times, if necessary. And if the teacher becomes angry and disturbed, the student should say, "My teacher, this is Torah, and I must learn it, but my capacities are limited."

Maimonides Mishna Torah,
Laws of Torah Study 4:4

6. A student should not be embarrassed if a fellow student has understood something on the first or second time and he has not grasped it even after a number of attempts. If he is embarrassed because of this, it will turn out that he will have spent his time in the house of study without learning anything at all.

Shulchan Aruch,
Yoreh De'ah 246:11

7. People should not go to study with a teacher who does not walk in the good way—even though he might be a great sage and might be needed by the people. They must not study with him until he reforms his ways.

Shulchan Aruch
Yoreh De'ah 246:8

8. People should first learn Torah-texts under the supervision of a teacher. Only afterwards should they begin to apply their own powers of reason, logic, and analogy.

Avoda Zara 19a
(with Rashi)

9. Rava said:

If there are two teachers available for hire—one who has studied extensively but is not meticulous about mistakes, and another who is meticulous about mistakes but has not studied as much, we hire the one who has studied extensively but is not as meticulous because mistakes have a way of working themselves out.

Rav Dimi of Neharde'a said:

We hire the one who is meticulous about mistakes, because once a mistake enters the students' minds, it stays there.

Bava Batra 21a

10. A person who reviews his subject matter one hundred times does not achieve the same understanding as a person who reviews it one hundred and one times.

Chagiga 9b

11. Rabbi Preda had a certain student to whom he had to teach everything four hundred times. One day, Rabbi Preda was going to be needed for a Mitzvah related to Tzedakah. He taught the student, but the student could not grasp the material.

He asked, "What is the matter?"

The student answered, "From the moment they said to you there is a Mitzvah to be done, I could not concentrate because I thought, 'Now he will have to go. Now he will have to go.'"

Rabbi Preda said to him, "Pay attention, and I will teach you again." He then reviewed the material another four hundred times.

A Voice from Heaven was heard to say to Rabbi Preda, "Would you prefer to have four hundred years added to your life, or that you and your entire generation be assured life in the World to Come?"

He answered, "May my generation and I be privileged to enter the World to Come."

The Holy One, blessed be He, said, "Give him both rewards."

Eruvin 54b

12. Rabbi Abbahu said:

The entire forty days that Moses was On High, he would study the Torah and then forget it.

He said, "Master of the world, I have been here forty days, and I know nothing."

What did the Holy One, blessed be He, do?

At the end of the forty days He gave Moses the Torah as a gift.

Exodus Rabba, Ki Tissa 41:6

13. Our rabbis have taught:

A person's Rebbi [Quintessential Teacher] is defined as one who teaches him wisdom, and not one who taught him the Written and the Oral Torah. This is Rabbi Meir's opinion.

Rabbi Yehudah says:

Whoever has taught him most of his wisdom.

Rabbi Yossi says:

Even if he did no more than make is eyes light up from an explanation of a single selection from the Oral Torah—he is still considered to be his Rebbi.

Bava Metzia 33a

14. Rabbi Akiva said:

I once followed my teacher, Rabbi Yehoshua, into the bathroom and learned three things about personal care from him. . . .

Ben Azzai said to Rabbi Akiva:

How could you dare to do such a thing with your teacher?

He said to him:

This, too, is Torah, and I needed to learn.

Berachot 62a

15. "And acquire a friend for yourself." (*Pirke Avot 1:6*)

How may this be accomplished?

A person should find another who will eat with him, drink with him, study the Written and Oral Torah with him, sleep with him, and reveal all his secrets to him—both the secrets of the Torah and the secrets of the ways of the world.

Avot DeRabbi Natan A:8

16. Whenever Rabbi Yoshiah and Rabbi Mattiah ben Cheresh would study Torah together, they studied with great passion. And when they parted, they treated each other like childhood friends.

Avot DeRabbi Natan A:1

17. One who reports a statement of Torah he has heard from someone else should imagine that person standing in front of him as he speaks.

Jerusalem Talmud,
Shabbat 1:2

18. Solomon did not only survey the words of Torah, but rather, "everything that was done under the heavens." (*Ecclesiastes 1:13*) He even investigated how to sweeten mustard and lupine-plants.

Song of Songs Rabba 1:1, Section 7

19. It was said that Rabban Yochanan ben Zakkai's studies included the following:

Bible, Mishna, Gemara [explication of the Mishna], legal and homiletical material, the intricacies of the Written and Oral Torah, various rules of Torah-logic, astronomy, arithmetic, washer's proverbs, fox fables, the languages of demons, palm trees, and angels, and great and small matters. "Great matters" refers to the study of God's divine chariot, and "small matters" refers to the intricate legal discussions between Rava and Abayye.

Bava Batra 134a

20. People can learn Torah well only if the material at hand is of particular interest to them.

Avoda Zara 19a

21. From what age should a parent begin to teach his child?

From the moment he begins to speak.

He begins by teaching him, "Moses instructed us in Torah, the heritage of the congregation of Jacob," (Deuteronomy 33:4) and the first verse of the Shema.

Afterwards he teaches him little by little until he is six or seven, and then takes him to a school for elementary Torah studies.

Shulchan Aruch,
Yoreh De'ah 245:5

22. When a child knows how to speak, his parent should teach him the Shema, Torah, and Hebrew, and if he does not do so, it were better that the child were not even born.

Tosefta Chagiga 1:1

23. "In his sickness, You have overturned his bed." (*Psalm 41:4*)

Rav Yosef said, "This means that he forgets his studies."

Rav Yosef himself became ill and forgot his Torah-knowledge, but Abayye re-taught it to him.

This is the meaning of the frequently mentioned statement that Rav Yosef made time and again, "I have not heard this law,"—and Abayye would remind him, "But you yourself taught it to us, deriving it from such-and-such a source."

Nedarim 41a

24. The question was raised:

Does a person who feeds another have to wash his hands or not?

Shmuel's father once found Shmuel crying.

He asked him, "Why are you crying?"

"Because my teacher hit me."

"Why did he do that?"

"Because he said to me, 'You were feeding my son and did not wash your hands before doing so.'"

Shmuel's father asked, "And why did you not wash?"

Shmuel replied, "It was he who was eating, so why should I wash?"

His father said, "It is not enough that the teacher does not know the law, but he also hit you!"

Chulin 107b

25. It is taught:

Every day an angel goes forth from the presence of the Blessed One, setting out to destroy the world—to return it to its primeval chaos.

However, when the Blessed One sees young children studying with their teachers, and the students of the wise sitting in their houses of study, his anger immediately changes to mercy.

Kallah Rabbati 2

26. Rabbi Shimon bar Yochai said:

Moses would show respect to Aaron by saying, "Teach me," and Aaron would show similar respect to Moses by saying, "Teach me." As a result, God's words came from between them, and it was as if both of them were speaking.

Mechilta,
Massechta d'Pischa 3
Lauterbach I:23

27. It was said of Yonatan ben Uzziel that, whenever he would sit to study Torah, any bird that flew overhead would be instantly incinerated.

Sukkah 28a

28. "Surrounded by lilies" (*Song of Songs 7:3*):

This refers to the words of Torah.
They are as delicate as lilies.

Song of Songs Rabba 7

29. Rabbi Mana said:

"It (Torah) is not an empty thing for you. It is your life."
(Deuteronomy 32:47)

If it is empty, it is because of you.

Why is that so? Because you do not work at it.

"It is your life. . . ." When is it your life? When you work hard at it.

Jerusalem Talmud,
Ketubot 8:11

30. Rabbi Shefatyah said in the name of Rabbi Yochanan:

The verse—"I gave them laws which were not good" (Ezekiel 20:25)— refers to someone who studies the Written Torah without the appropriate melody, and studies the Oral Torah without a tune.

Megillah 32a

HUMAN QUALITIES

31. In life, you discover that people are called by three names:

One is the name the person is called by his father and mother; one is the name people call him, and one is the name he acquires for himself.

The best one is the one he acquires for himself.

Tanchuma, Vayakhel, 1

32. Rabbi Ila'i said:

A person may be known by three things—
by his cup,
by his pocket,
and by his anger.
And some say:
Also by his laughter.

Eruvin 65b

33. When Rabbi Meir died, the last great fable-teller died.
When Ben Azzai died, the last ultra-diligent student died.
When Ben Zoma died, the last great sermonizer died.
When Rabbi Yehoshua died, goodness left the world.
When Rabban Shimon ben Gamliel died, locusts came and troubles
    increased.
When Rabbi Elazar ben Azaryah died, great wealth ceased among the
    sages.
When Rabbi Akiva died, the glory of the Torah ceased.
When Rabbi Chanina ben Dosa died, great wonder-workers were no
    more.
When Rabbi Yossi Ketanta died, true piety ceased. . . . for he embodied
    the essence of the pious.
When Rabban Yochanan ben Zakkai died, the radiance of wisdom
    ceased.
When Rabban Gamliel the Elder died, the glory of the Torah ceased
    and purity and abstinence passed away.
When Rabbi Yishmael ben Pavi died, the radiance of the priesthood
    ceased.
When Rabbi Yehuda the Prince died, humility and the fear of sin
    ceased.

Mishna Sota 9, End

34. Rabbah the son of Rava (and some say: Rabbi Hillel the son of Rabbi Vallas said):

From the days of Moses until Rabbi Yehudah the Prince we have not found Torah and greatness in one place.

Sanhedrin 36a

35. Take note:

Even though the House of Shammai and the House of Hillel often disagreed on important matters, this did not prevent them from marrying members of each other's circle.

Yevamot 14b

36. Rabbah the son of Rav Huna said:

It is permitted to call an arrogant person "evil."

Rav Nachman the son of Yitzchak said:

It is permitted to hate him.

Ta'anit 7b

37. Rav Yehuda said in Rav's name:

Whoever is arrogant—
if he is a sage, he will lose his wisdom;
if he is a prophet, he will lose his power of prophecy.

Pesachim 66b

38. The townspeople of Simoniah came to Rabbi Yehuda HaNassi and said, "We would like to hire someone who can interpret Torah for us, judge us, supervise our synagogue affairs, teach us elementary and advanced Torah, and oversee whatever might be our needs."

He gave them Levi Bar Sisi.

The Simonians made him a large Bima, sat him upon it, and approached him with a question of Halacha.

He gave no answer.

They asked him another such question, and, again, he did not reply. They said, "Perhaps he is not an expert in Halacha. Let us ask him to explain a verse from the Book of Daniel."

They did so, but, still, he had no answer for them.

They went back to Rabbi Yehuda HaNassi and said, "Is this the way you satisfy our request?"

He replied, "I swear I have given you someone as good as myself. Bring him here."

Rabbi Yehuda asked him the same three questions, and he immediately gave substantial, appropriate answers.

So Rabbi Yehuda asked, "Why did you not answer them when they asked?"

He replied, "They made me this huge Bima and sat me upon it, and I became so enthralled by my own self-importance, I could not function properly.

Jerusalem Talmud,
Yevamot 12:6

SENSITIVITY

39. We are taught:

If the eye only had the power to see, no one could survive because of the Evil Spirits.

Berachot 6a

40. Rabbi Yossi says,

"Woe to God's creatures who see and do not know what they see!"

Chagiga 12b

41. Our rabbis have taught:

Seven things are hidden from human beings—the day of death, the day of comfort, the extent of judgment; one human being does not know what is in another's heart, nor does he know from what he will earn a living, nor when the Kingdom of David will return, nor when the Evil Kingdom will end.

Pesachim 54b

42. Three kinds of people live lives that are not really living:
Oversensitive people,
irascible people,
and physically delicate people.

Pesachim 113b

43. Rabbi Yannai says:

"All the days of the poor are bad" (*Proverbs 15:15*)—
This refers to a person who is physically delicate.
"But one with a good heart has an eternal feast" (*Proverbs 15:15*)—
This refers to a person who has a hardy constitution.

Rabbi Yochanan says:

"All the days of the poor are bad" (*Proverbs 15:15*)—
This refers to a person who is compassionate.
"But one with a good heart has an eternal feast (*Proverbs 15:15*)—
This refers to a person who is cruel.

Bava Batra 145b

MONEY

44. We are taught:

Who is to be considered truly wealthy?

He who derives peace of mind from his wealth. This is the opinion of Rabbi Meir.

Rabbi Tarfon says: He who has a hundred vineyards, a hundred fields, and a hundred workers working in them.

Rabbi Akiva says: He who has a spouse who does exquisite deeds.

Rabbi Yossi says: He who has a bathroom near his diningroom table.

Shabbat 25b

45. The One Who has created the day has also created the means for a living.

Rabbi Elazar used to say:

Whoever has enough to eat for today and says, "What will I eat tomorrow?" is a person of little faith.

Mechilta,
Massechta DeVayissa 3
Lauterbach II: 103

46. Rabbi Yishmael said:

One who wishes to acquire wisdom should study the way money works, for there is no greater area of Torah-study than this. It is like an ever-flowing stream. And one who wishes to study money matters should apprentice himself to Rabbi Shimon ben Nannas.

Bava Batra 175b

47. Rabbi Yochanan was once robbed by a gang of thieves. When he went into the Study House, Resh Lakish asked him a question, but he did not respond. He asked him another, but, again, he did not answer.

Resh Lakish asked him, "What's wrong?"

Rabbi Yochanan answered, "All the parts of the body depend on the heart, and the heart depends on the pocket."

"What happened?"

"I was robbed by thieves."

"Which way did they go?"

He showed Resh Lakish which way they had gone, and when Resh Lakish saw them from a distance, he screamed at them.

The thieves said, "If it is Rabbi Yochanan's money, we will return half of it."

Resh Lakish said, "If you value your lives, I will take it all back." He then took it all back from them.

Jerusalem Talmud,
Terumot 8:4

48. Alexander the Great once stood at the door of the Garden of Eden and shouted, "Open the gate for me."

They replied, "This is the gate of the Lord, only the righteous are entitled to enter." (*Psalm 118:20*)

He said, "I am a king. I am someone of great importance. Give me something."

They gave him an eyeball.

He weighed all his silver and gold against it, but they did not weigh as much.

He said to the rabbis, "What is the meaning of all this?"

They replied, "This is a human eyeball, which is never satisfied."

He asked, "How do you know this is true?"

They took a little dust and covered it. It was immediately weighed down.

Tamid 32b

49. Rabbi Akiva said to his wife, "If I only had the means, I would buy you a Jerusalem of gold."

Nedarim 50a

50. Rabbi Yudan has said in the name of Rabbi Aibo:

People never leave this world with half their cravings satisfied.

If they have a hundred, they want two hundred, and if they have two hundred, they want four hundred.

Ecclesiastes Rabba 3:12

51. Rabbi Natan bar Abba said in the name of Rav, "The wealthy of Babylonia deserve to go to Hell!

"See, for example, when Shabbetai bar Maraynus came to Babylonia—he looked for help in setting up a business, but they did not help. And even when he asked for help for food, they did not give him any."

Betzah 32b

52. Rabbi Yehuda used to say:

Ten strong things were created in the world—
A mountain is strong, but iron cuts through it.
Iron is strong, but fire causes it to bubble.
Fire is strong, but water extinguishes it.
Water is strong, but clouds contain it.
Clouds are strong, but the wind (ruach) scatters them.
Breath (ruach) is strong, but the body holds it in.
The body is strong, but fear breaks it.
Fear is strong, but wine dissipates its effects.
Wine is strong, but sleep overcomes its power.
Death is harder than all of them.
But Tzedakah saves from death, as it is written,
"And Tzedakah saves from death." (*Proverbs 10:2*)

Bava Batra 10a

53. It was taught in the name of Rabbi Yehoshua:

The poor person [standing at the door] does more for the householder than the householder does for the poor person.

Leviticus Rabba 34:8

54. Rabbi Abba bar Acha said:

It is impossible to understand the nature of this people—
when they are asked to contribute to the Golden Calf,
they give,
and when they are asked to contribute to the building of
the Tabernacle,
they give.

Shekalim 1:1

THE ANGEL

55. While the fetus is still in the womb, it is taught the entire Torah. As it emerges into the air of this world, an angel comes and slaps it on the mouth, making it forget all the Torah it had learned. It does not leave the womb until it is made to take an oath. And what is this oath?

"Be righteous and do not be wicked.

And even if the whole world calls you righteous, do not consider yourself to be what they say.

Know that the Holy One, blessed be He, is pure, and His servants are pure, and the soul which He has given to you is pure. If you preserve its purity—fine. If not, it will be taken away from you."

Then the Holy One, blessed be He, summons the angel who is in charge of souls and says, "Bring me So-and-So's soul." The soul immediately comes before the Holy One, blessed be He, and bows before Him.

The Holy One, blessed be he, says to it, "Enter this drop." The soul then says, "Master of the World, since I was created, this world has been good to me. If it is all right with You, please do not put me into this stinking drop, because I am holy and pure."

The Holy One, blessed be He, says to the soul, "The world which you will enter is better than this world, and, besides, when I created you, I only created you for this drop."

The Holy One, blessed be He, then forces the soul into the drop, and the angel returns the drop, with the soul, into the mother's womb. He also stations two angels there to prevent miscarriages.

A candle sits on its head, and by its light the developing fetus sees from one end of the world to the other.

In the morning, the angel takes it on a tour of the Garden of Eden, showing it the Righteous sitting in great majesty.

The angel says, "Do you know whose soul that one is?"

"No," he replies.

The angel says, "The one you see there treated with such honor and majesty was created just like you in the mother's womb. And this one, and that one, too. And they kept God's way carefully. If you do as they did, then, after your death, as after theirs, you will be privileged to enjoy all this grandeur and this honor—just as you see it now. But if you do not act that way, you will find yourself in another place. . . . which I will show you.

In the evening, he takes it to Gehinnom and shows it wicked people being beaten with fiery clubs by angels of destruction. They are screaming, "Oy V'avoi!" No mercy is shown to them.

The angel says, "My child, do you know who these people are who are being burned?"

And he answers, "No, I do not."

The angel responds, "Know that these, too, were created from a stinking drop in the mother's womb. They entered the world, but did not keep the ways of the Holy One, blessed be He. That is why they have been reduced to such degradation."

The angel takes him around to every place where he will ever be, and to his future home, and to where he will be buried, and then takes him back to the womb.

Then the Holy One, blessed be He, sets up double doors and a cross-bar to the womb and says, "For now, you may go only this far—no farther."

When it is time for the fetus to be born, the same angel comes and says, "Go! Your time to be born has arrived."

But the fetus says, "But have I not already told the Holy One, blessed be He, "I am satisfied in the world where I am'?"

The angel replies, "The world I am taking you into is beautiful. Furthermore, whether you wanted it or not, you were created, and, against your will, you will be born."

At the moment of birth, the infant weeps.

Why does he weep?

He weeps for that world he is leaving.

And he weeps because, at that moment, they show him seven worlds: In the first world, he is like a king—everyone looks after him and runs to see him, and hugs and kisses him. . . . until he is a year old.

In the second world, he is like a pig—always in the garbage, and a mess to clean. . . . until he is two.

In the third world, he is like a baby goat dancing in the meadow—always dancing everywhere. . . . until he is five.

In the fourth world, he is like a horse, proudly prancing down the road—this is what a child is like, full of pride and sure of the powers of youth. . . . until he is eighteen.

In the fifth world, he is like a mule with a saddle on his back—with a wife and sons and daughters, running around looking for a livelihood to support the members of his household.

In the sixth world, he is like a dog, still grabbing for a livelihood wherever he can, sometimes being pushy, taking and stealing from one and then others without shame.

In the seventh world, he does not resemble anything, having become different from all other things—even his family curses him and wishes he were dead, and even infants make fun of him.

Finally, when his time comes to die, the angel comes to him and says, "Do you recognize me?"

And he answers, "Yes. but why have you come to me today?"

The angel answers, "To take you away from this world."

He weeps deeply—a weeping that can be heard around the world, though no human being can hear it—and he says to the angel, "Have you not already taken me from two worlds and put me in this one?"

And the angel replies, "But have I not already told you, 'Against your will you were created, and were born, and will die, and will—against your will—give an accounting to the King of Kings of Kings, the Holy One Blessed be He'?"

Niddah 30b,
Seder Yetzirat HaVelad,
Bet Hamidrash I:153–155

HEAVEN AND HELL

56. The sun is red at sunrise because it passes by the roses of the Garden of Eden, and at sunset because it passes by the gate of Hell.

Bava Batra 84a

57. In Elijah's academy it was taught:

Hell is above the sky. Some say it is behind the Mountains of Darkness.

Tamid 32b

58. Rabbi Yirmiah ben Elazar said:

There are three doors to Hell—one in the desert, one in the sea, and one in Jerusalem.

Eruvin 19a

59. A certain caravan merchant once said to Rabbah bar bar Channah, "Come, I will show you the place where heaven and earth touch so closely it appears that they are kissing."

Bava Batra 74a

PRAYING

60. The Holy One, blessed be He, said to the Jews:

I have said to you—
When you pray, pray in the synagogue in your city.
If you cannot pray in the synagogue, pray in your field.
If you cannot pray in your field, pray in your house.
And if you cannot pray in your house, pray on your bed.
And if you cannot pray on your bed, reflect in your heart.

Midrash on Psalms 4:9

61. Rabbi Chiyya bar Abba said in the name of Rabbi Yochanan:

One should only pray in a house where there are windows.

Berachot 34b

62. One who is praying should keep his eyes turned down and his heart turned up.

Yevamot 105b

TORAH AND LIFE

63. What is an example of a foolish religious person?

When a woman is drowning in the river, and he says, "It is not proper for me to look at her . . . so I cannot save her."

Sotah 21b

64. What is an example of a foolish religious person?

One who sees a child bobbing up and down in the river and says, "Once I get my Tfillin off, I will save him. . . ."—by the time he removes his Tfillin, the child will have drowned.

Jersualem Talmud,
Sotah 3:4

65. Rabbi Tarfon said,

"Akiva, whoever separates himself from you—it is as though he disconnects himself from Life itself."

Kiddushin 66b

66. Rabbi Tarfon said,

"Akiva, whoever separates himself from you—it is as though he disconnects himself from his own life."

Zevachim 13a

67. Rabbi Yehuda said:

One who would wish to become a saintly person should live the words of Nezikin [The Talmudic material on damages and interpersonal relations.]

Rava said:

The words of Avot [the Talmudic selection called, "Sayings of the Fathers."]

And some say [he said]:

The words of Brachot [the Talmudic material concerning blessings.]

Bava Kamma 30a

APHORISMS
and other Brief Insights

68. In Rabbi Shayla's academy it was taught:

Whoever avoids evil is considered by others to be a fool.

Sanhedrin 97a

69. The greater the person, the greater the inclination to do wrong.

Sukkah 52a

70. Honor your doctor before you need him.

Jerusalem Talmud,
Ta'anit 3:6

71. Only a portion of another's praise may be offered in his presence, though all of it may be stated in his absence.

Eruvin 18b

72. At times, adding on detracts.

Sanhedrin 29a

73. A person should use his face, hands, and feet only to honor his Creator.

Tosefta Brachot 4:1

74. Eat quickly, drink quickly, for the world we leave is like a wedding feast.

Eruvin 54a

75. Our Rabbis have taught:

It is prohibited to enjoy anything in this world without a Bracha.

Berachot 35a

76. Tongs are made with other tongs. Who, then, made the first tongs?

Pesachim 54a

77. Rabbah bar Bar Channah said in Rabbi Yochanan's name in the name of Rabbi Yehuda bar Ha'i:

Eat onions and live in your own house, and do not eat geese and fowl so that your heart pursues you. Eat and drink less, but spend more on your home.

Pesachim 114a

78. If you spit into the air, it will fall on your face.

Ecclesiastes Rabba 7:21

79. Sixty runners may run after you, but they will not catch up with you if you have eaten an early breakfast.

Though a duck walks low to the ground, its eyes sweep great distances.

'A person's tooth feels sixty toothaches when he hears another eating but he himself does not eat.

Don't throw clods of dirt into a well from which you have drunk.

Bava Kamma 92b

80. There are many old camels bearing the hides of young camels on their backs.

Sanhedrin 52a

81. Even among thorns a willow is still called a willow.

Sanhedrin 44a

82. When our love was strong, we could have slept on the blade of a sword. Now that our love is no longer strong, a bed sixty cubits wide is not large enough for us.

Sanhedrin 7a

83. A folk saying goes:

She whores for apples, then gives them to the sick.

Leviticus Rabba 3:1

A MISCELLANY

84. Rabbi Abbahu was sitting and teaching in one of the synagogues in Caesarea. He noticed a man carrying a stick who was about to hit someone. Behind that man he saw a demon carrying an iron club. Rabbi Abbahu immediately got up and appealed to the man, saying, "Do you want to kill this man?"

The man replied, "With a stick like this, can anyone kill anyone else?"

Rabbi Abbahu answered, "There is a demon standing behind you with an iron club in his hands. If you hit the man with your stick, he will hit him from the other side with his club, and the man will die."

Lamentations Rabba 1:30

85. Rabbi Yehoshua said:

Always consider others as if they were thieves, but honor them as if they were as great as Rabban Gamliel.

Derech Eretz Rabba 5

86. Rava bar Mechasia said in the name of Chama bar Goria who said in the name of Rav:

One should never show favoritism among one's children, for because of two coins' worth of fine wool that Jacob gave to Joseph beyond what he gave to the other sons—the brothers became jealous, and one thing led to another until our ancestors became slaves in Egypt.

Shabbat 10b

87. Rabbi Yossi bar Chanina said:

During the second plague, the croaking was worse than the frogs themselves.

Pesikta deRav Kahana 7:11

88. "And when the Lord has brought you into the land of the Canaanites, as He swore to you and your fathers, and has given it to you. . . ."
(*Exodus 13:11*)

The Land should not be thought of as an inheritance from your ancestors, but rather as if it were given to *you* this very day.

Mechilta, Massechta d'Pischa 18
Lauterbach I:159

89. Do not be troubled with tomorrow's woes because you do not know what the day will bring forth. It may be that tomorrow will come, and you will be no more and you will have troubled yourself about a world which is not yours. (Ben Sira)

Yevamot 63b

90. Rav Chizkiya or Rav Cohen said in the name of Rav:

In the Future, everyone will have to give an accounting for everything his eyes saw, but of which he did not eat. Rabbi Le'azar paid particular attention to this statement, setting aside money so that he could eat every kind of food at least once a year.

Jerusalem Talmud,
Kiddushin 4, end

91. Rabbah said:

When the Rabbis in Pumpeditha would take leave of each other, they would recite the following—

"May He Who gives life to the living give you a long, good, and stable life."

Yoma 71a

92. A person should not be awake among those who are asleep,
nor asleep among those who are awake,
nor weeping among those who are laughing,
nor laughing among those who are weeping,
nor sitting among those who are standing,
nor standing among those who are sitting,
nor reading the Written Torah among those studying the Oral Torah,
nor reading the Oral Torah among those studying the Written Torah.

Derech Eretz Zuta 5

93. Rabbi Ila'i said in the name of Rabbi Elazar the son of Rabbi Shimon:

Just as it is a Mitzvah to say something which will be listened to, so, too,
is it a Mitzvah not to say something which will not be listened to.

Yevamot 65b

94. Rabbi Chiyya bar Abba became ill.
Rabbi Yochanan went to visit him.
He said, "Do you appreciate your suffering?"
He replied, "Neither the suffering nor any reward I might receive
     for the suffering."
Rabbi Yochanan said, "Give me your hand."
He gave him his hand and Rabbi Yochanan raised him from his sickbed.

Berachot 5b

95. One who would wish to sense the delicate beauty of Rabbi Yochanan
should take a silver goblet—just at the moment the silversmith has
finished polishing it—fill it with the seeds of a red pomegranate, circle
its brim with a crown of red roses, and set it between the sunlight and
the shade. That radiance resembles the beauty of Rabbi Yochanan.

Bava Metzia 84a

96. Rabbi Shimon bar Yochai said:

Had I stood at Mount Sinai at the moment the Torah was being given, I would have asked the Merciful God to create two mouths for people—one for Torah and the other for day-to-day needs.

Later on he said:

I see now that the world struggles so much to survive when people have only one mouth—because of their outrageous slander. How much worse it would be if they had two mouths!

Jerusalem Talmud,
Shabbat 1:2

97. Rav Chanan bar Rav said:

Everyone knows why a bride enters the Chuppah, but, nevertheless, anyone who speaks obscenely of the event—even if he were entitled by Heaven to seventy good years—all that good will be turned into misfortune.

Ketubot 8b

98. Rabbi Pinchas said:

It once happened that two prostitutes from Ashkelon were arguing with each other. In the course of the argument one of them said to the other, "You should not go out on the streets because you have a Jewish face!"

A few days later, after they had settled their differences, the second prostitute said, "I forgive you for everything you said except for your snide remark that I have a Jewish face." This is the meaning of the verse, "See, O God, how despicable I have become." (Lamentations 1:11)

Lamentations Rabba 1:41

99. We are taught:

[The High Priest] would recite a brief prayer in the outer enclosure of the Temple.

What would he say?

Rabin bar Ada and Rava bar Ada said in the name of Rav Yehuda, "May it be Your will, O Lord, our God, that if this year will be a hot one, let it also be rainy and filled with dew, and do not listen to the prayers of travellers."

Ta'anit 24b

100. Whoever sees a rainbow in the clouds should fall on his face in awe, as the verse says, "The appearance of the brilliance was like the appearance of a rainbow in the clouds on a rainy day—that was the likeness of God's Glory that I saw, and I fell on my face [and heard a voice speaking.]" (Ezekiel 1:28)

Berachot 59a

101. When Rav Yosef would hear the footsteps of his mother, he would say, "I shall arise before God's approaching Presence."

Kiddushin 31b

102. Rabbi Yochanan said in the name of Rabbi Shimon ben Yehotzadak:

A community leader may not be appointed unless he has a basket of unclean reptiles hanging over his back, so that if he becomes arrogant, he can be told, "Just turn around!"

Yoma 22b

103. When a person goes to the bathroom, he says [to the two angels that are always with him],

"Guard me, guard me. Help me, help me. Be reliable, be reliable. Wait for me, wait for me, until I go in and come out—for this is what human beings have to do."

Berachot 60b

104. Rabbi Nathan said:

Jonah went down to the sea in order to drown himself.

Mechilta, Massechta d'Pischa
Lauterbach I:10

105. A wise person [Talmid Chacham] is not permitted to live in a city that does not have the following ten things:

1. A court empowered to punish the guilty
2. A communal Tzedakah fund, monies for which are collected by two people and distributed by three
3. A synagogue
4. A bath house
5. Sufficient bathroom facilities
6. A doctor
7. A blood-letter
8. A scribe
9. A butcher
10. A Torah teacher for children

It was stated in Rabbi Akiva's name:

Also, a variety of fruits, because a variety of fruits brightens the eyes.

Sanhedrin 17b

CHILDREN

106. Rabbi Abbahu said, "Though a baby emerges from its mother's womb covered with mucus and blood, everyone hugs and kisses it."

Leviticus Rabba 14:4

107. We are taught:

After a child would be born on Shabbat, the wealthy would store the placenta in oil, and the poor would store it in straw and sand. After Shabbat, both would bury it in the earth, as a guarantee to the earth.

Jerusalem Talmud,
Shabbat 18:3

108. Rabbi Yochanan said:

Since the time of the destruction of the Temple, prophecy has been taken away from the prophets and given over to fools and infants.

Bava Batra 12b

109. Rabbi Yochanan said in the name of Rabbi Yossi ben Katzarta:

There are six kinds of tears—
three are beneficial, and three are harmful.
Tears caused by smoke, weeping from grief, and straining in the bathroom are harmful.
Tears caused by certain chemicals, laughter, and certain plants [such as onions and mustard] are beneficial.
Tears from laughter are the best of all;
tears from the death of a child are the worst of all.

Shabbat 151b–152a
Lamentations Rabba 2:19

OLD AGE

110. Rabbi Yossi ben Kisma says:

Two are better than three.
Woe for the one that leaves us and does not return.
What is that?

Rav Chisda said: our youth.
When Rav Dimi came from Israel, he said:
Youth is a crown of roses.
Old age is a crown of thorns.

Shabbat 152a

111. When we were young, we were told to act like adults.
Now that we are old, we are treated like infants.

Bava Kamma 92b

112. It was said of Rabbi Chanina that at the age of eighty he could still stand on one foot and remove and replace the shoe on his other foot.

Rabbi Chanina said, "The warm baths and oil with which my mother rubbed me have served me well in my old age."

Chullin 24b

113. One who is delivering a divorce document for someone who is old—even 100 years old—still delivers it with the assumption that the man is alive. . . . since, if he has lived so long, he is bound to continue living longer.

Gittin 28a

114. "A man went from the land of the Hittites and built a city. He called it Luz, and that is its name to this very day." (Judges 1:26) We are taught. . . . :

The Angel of Death does not have permission to go there. When the old no longer wish to go on living, they go outside the city walls and die.

Sotah 46b

MARRIAGE AND DIVORCE

115. Rabbi Yossi HaGlili's wife caused him great anguish.

Rabbi Elazar ben Azariah went to visit him and said, "Divorce her, because she does not treat you with dignity."

He said to him, "But I cannot afford to pay the settlement."

He said, "I will pay it for you. Just divorce her."

Rabbi Elazar ben Azariah paid the settlement for him, and he divorced his wife.

She eventually married one of the town guards who later became poor and blind. She would lead him around town begging for money.

Once, she took him through the entire town without finding any money.

He said to her, "Are there any other neighborhoods where we have not been?"

She said, "There is one neighborhood left, but I do not have the strength to go there."

He began to beat her, just as Rabbi Yossi HaGlili was passing by.

He heard her shouts and saw the way she was being humiliated.

Because of this, he took them in and gave them accomodations in one of his houses and provided for them for the rest of their lives.

Jerusalem Talmud,
Ketubot 11:3

116. Rabbi Iddi said:

Once upon a time a certain woman in Tzidon was married to a certain man, but they had no children. They came to Rabbi Shimon bar Yochai and requested a divorce.

He said, "By your lives, just as you were married in the midst of a great feast, so, too, shall you begin your separation with a great feast."

They followed his instructions and made a feast. During the meal the woman gave the man too much to drink. As he began to get sober he said, "My beloved, survey all the precious things in this house, take that which is most dear to you, and return to your father's house."

What did she do?

After he fell asleep, she told her servants, "Carry him on his bed to my father's house."

In the middle of the night, he awoke, and, as he became more sober, he asked, "My beloved, where am I?"

She said, "In my father's house."

He asked, "What am I doing in your father's house?"

She said, "Did you not say to me this evening, 'Choose whatever is most precious to you and take it with you to your father's house'? There is nothing more precious to me in the entire world than you."

They then went back to Rabbi Shimon bar Yochai, who prayed for them, and they had children.

Song of Songs,
Rabba to 1:14, Nagilah

OUR SOULS

117. Rabbi Alexandri said:

When you leave new things in a human being's possession for safe-keeping, though they might have been new when they were delivered, they are often returned used and worn out.

The Holy One, blessed be He, though, works differently:

Though we leave things in His hand all worn out and tattered,
He returns them to us new.

This is obvious to us—

a worker will work all day and come home exhausted;
when he is asleep, though, he is at peace, since his soul is in the hands of the Holy One, blessed be He.

Indeed, at dawn, the soul returns, a new creation to the worker's body, as the verse indicates, "[Souls] are new every morning; great is Your reliability." (Lamentations 3:23)

Midrash on Psalms 25:2

118. "To You, O Lord, I lift my soul." (Psalm 25:1)

This verse may be understood by referring to the words, "Into Your hand I entrust my spirit." (Psalm 31:6)

This is the way of the world:

If one leaves some items for another to watch, sometimes the latter mixes them up with someone else's possessions for some objects are not easily distinguishable from others. But the Holy One, blessed be He, does not work that way, but, rather, "God is a God of truth." (Psalm 31:6)

Has anyone ever awakened in the morning and looked for his soul and not found it? Or has anyone ever found his soul in another's possession or another's in his possession? "You redeem me, O Lord, reliable God." (Psalm 31:6)

Midrash on Psalms 25:2

THE CREATOR

119. "There is no rock (*Tzur*) like our God." (I Samuel 2:2)

There is no artist (*Tzayyar*) like our God:

A human being can cut a form on a wall but cannot make breath, a soul, organs or intestines for it. But the Holy One, blessed be He, fashions forms within forms and gives them breath, a soul, and all the organs needed for life.

Megillah 14a

120. "There is no rock (*Tzur*) like our God." (I Samuel 2:2)

There is no artist (*Tzayyar*) like our God.

This is the way of human beings:

A person goes to a sculptor and says, "Make a statue of my father for me."

The sculptor says, "Let your father come to pose for me, or bring me some image of him."

But the One Who spoke and brought the world into being is different:

He gives a person a child formed from a drop of fluid, and it resembles the parent.

Mechilta Shirata 8
Lauterbach II:65

121. God and human beings do not act the same:

The creations of human beings outlive them, but the Holy One, blessed be He, outlives His creations.

Megillah 14a

122. "Awesome in splendor, working wonders!" (Exodus 15:11)
Human beings function in the following manner:

A worker works for his landowner, plowing, sowing, weeding, and hoeing for him, and his employer gives him money, and he goes his way.

It is different, however, with the One Who spoke and created the world thereby:

If a person desires children, He can give them to him; if he desires wisdom, He can give it to him; possessions, He can give them to him.

Mechilta, Shirata 8
Lauterbach II:63–64

123. You have confused the creation with its creator.

Deuteronomy Rabba 1:3

SHABBAT

124. Rabbi Shimon ben Lakish said:

Before Shabbat begins, the Holy One, blessed be He, gives every person an additional soul, and when Shabbat is over, it is taken back from him.

Betzah 16a

125. Your Shabbat clothes should not be the same as your weekday clothes.

Shabbat 113a

126. We are permitted to comfort mourners on Shabbat. So, too, are we allowed to visit the sick on Shabbat.

Shulchan Aruch,
Orach Chaim 287:1

127. We are permitted to weep on Shabbat if weeping is a pleasure because it releases pain in the heart.

Isserles, Shulchan Aruch,
Orach Chaim 288:2

128. The Jews have been assured that Elijah will not come on the eve of Shabbat nor on the eve of holidays.

Eruvin 43b

THE TROUBLES OF THE JEWS

129. Our teachers have said:

Once, while Moses, our Teacher, was tending Yitro's sheep, one of the sheep ran away. Moses ran after it until it reached a small, shaded place. There the lamb came across a pool of water and began to drink. As Moses approached the lamb, he said, "I did not know you ran away because you were thirsty. You are so exhausted!" He then put the lamb on his shoulders and carried him back.

The Holy One, blessed be He, said, "Since you tend the sheep of human beings with such overwhelming love—by your life, I swear you shall be the shepherd of My sheep, Israel."

Exodus Rabba 2:2

130. [*While Moses was tending the flocks of his father-in-law, Yitro, in Midian, God took note of Moses's concern for the anguish of the Children of Israel in Egypt.*]

The Holy One, blessed be He, said, "Since Moses is disheartened and troubled by the woes of Israel in Egypt, he is worthy to be their shepherd."

Exodus Rabba 2:6

131. When the Jews are in trouble, a person should not say, "I will go to my home, eat, drink, and be at peace with myself."

Ta'anit 11a

132. When the Jews are in trouble, and one individual distances himself from them, the two angels who always accompany everybody come and put their hands on that person's head and say, "This person who separated himself from the people shall not be entitled to witness the consolation of the people."

Ta'anit 11a

THE EXODUS

133. Only one out of five of the Children of Israel left Egypt.
Some say one out of fifty.
And some say only one out of five hundred.

Rabbi Nehorai says:
Not even one out of five hundred.

Mechilta, Massechta dePischa 12
Lauterbach

134. When the Israelites fled from Egypt, they were outnumbered three to one.
Some say thirty to one.
And some say three hundred to one.

Mechilta, Beshallach 2
Lauterbach

135. "They shall take some of the blood and put it on the two doorposts and on the lintel." (Exodus 12:7)

On the inside, as it says, "And I shall see the blood" (12:13). . . . the blood that I [the Lord] will see, and not the blood others will see.

These are the words of Rabbi Yishmael.

Rabbi Yonatan says:

On the inside, as it says, "And the blood shall be a sign for you."

Rabbi Yitzchak says:

It certainly means on the outside, so that the Egyptians would see it and be terrified.

Mechilta, Massechta dePischa 6
Lauterbach I:44

136. Once the Angel of Destruction is allowed to begin his work, he does not differentiate between the Righteous and the Wicked.

Mechilta, Massechta dePischa 11
Lauterbach I:85

137. At the Red Sea the Israelites divided into four factions:
One group said, "Let us throw ourselves into the sea."
Another said, "Let us go back to Egypt."
Another said, "Let us fight them."
And the fourth said, "Let us make a lot of noise [to scare them.]"

Mechilta, BeShallach 3
Lauterbach I:214

138. At the Red Sea the Egyptians divided into three factions:

One said, "Let us take their money and take back our money, but let us not kill them."

Another said, "Let us kill them but not take their money."

And the third said, "Let us kill them and take their money."

Mechilta Shirata 7
Lauterbach II:57

139. The Israelites saw the Egyptians dying on the seashore, but they did not see them dead.

Mechilta BeShallach 7
Lauterbach I:250

140. "The Lord said to Moses, 'Why do you cry out to me?'" (Exodus 14:15)

Rabbi Eliezer says:

The Holy One, blessed be He, said to Moses,

"Moses, my children are in mortal danger—the sea is on one side and the enemy is pursuing from the other—and you stand here and take time to say lengthy prayers? Why do you cry out to me?"

As Rabbi Eliezer used to say:

There are appropriate times for short prayers and appropriate times for long prayers.

Mechilta BeShallach 4
Lauterbach I:216

141. When the tribes stood at the shore of the Red Sea, they began to argue, each saying, "I will go in first!"

While they were arguing, the tribe of Benjamin jumped in first.

The leaders of the tribe of Judah then began to throw stones at them.

Mechilta BeShallach 6
Lauterbach I:232

142. Rabbi Yehuda ben Betayra says:

"But they would not listen to Moses, their spirits crushed." (Exodus 6:9)

Is it possible that someone would hear good news and not be overjoyed?—

"A son has been born to you. . . ."—and he should not be overjoyed?

"Your master is setting you free. . . ."—and he should not be overjoyed?

So why, then, should the Torah say, "They would not listen to Moses"? Because it was difficult for them to tear themselves away from their idols.

Mechilta, Massechta dePischa 5
Lauterbach I:38

143. Why did God speak to Moses outside of the city?

Because the city was filled with abominations and idols.

Mechilta, Massechta dePischa 1
Lauterbach I:4

REVOLT

144. During the three and a half years that Hadrian besieged Bethar during the Bar Kochba revolt, Rabbi Elazar of Modi'in dressed in sackcloth and sat in ashes, praying every day, "Master of all worlds, do not sit in judgment today! Do not sit in judgment today!"

Jerusalem Talmud,
Ta'anit 4:4

145. Rabbi Tzadok fasted for forty years so that Jerusalem might not be destroyed.

Gittin 56a

146. Rabbi Yehuda and Rabbi Yossi and Rabbi Shimon were sitting together, along with Rabbi Yehuda ben Gerim.

Rabbi Yehuda began the conversation, "What exquisite things Rome accomplishes! They have set up marketplaces, bridges, and bath houses!"

Rabbi Yossi remained silent.

Rabbi Shimon Bar Yochai replied,
"Whatever they do is only for selfish reasons.

They set up markets only to make a place for their whores.
They build bath houses only to pamper themselves.
They set up bridges only to collect tolls."

Shabbat 33b

147. When Rabbi Akiva would see Bar Kochba, he would say, "This is the King Messiah."

Rabbi Yochanan ben Torata said to him,

"Akiva—grass will grow from your cheeks before the Son of David will come."

Jerusalem Talmud,
Ta'anit 4:4

148. The Romans continued to slaughter the Jews until their horses sank to their snouts in blood. The blood gushed to such a degree that huge boulders rolled in the flow, and the blood washed all the way to the sea forty Roman miles away.

It was said that they found the brains of three hundred children splattered on one rock.

Jerusalem Talmud,
Ta'anit 4:4

149. For seven years after the Bar Kochba revolt, the Romans did not need fertilizer for their vineyards—because of all the Jewish blood that was spilled.

Gittin 57a

150. The Emperor Hadrian had a vineyard eighteen Roman miles square that he encircled with bodies from Bethar.

He would not allow them to be buried, until a new emperor rose to power and allowed them to be buried.

Lamentations Rabba 2:5

DEATH AND MOURNING

151. We are not permitted to leave a person who is near death, so that he should not have to die alone. And it is a Mitzvah to stand by a person at the moment of death.

Shulchan Aruch,
Yoreh De'ah 339:4

152. If we are in the presence of someone who is dying, we are required to tear our garment at the moment of death.

What is this like?

It is like a Sefer Torah that has been burned, an occasion for which we are also required to tear our garment.

Mo'ed Katan 25a

153. We may desecrate the Sabbath for a day-old infant, if he is still alive, but if he has already died, we may not do so even for someone as great as David, King of Israel.

Shabbat 151b

154. Rava said to Rav Nachman, "Show yourself to me [in a dream after you die]."

He showed himself to Rava.

Rava asked him, "Was death painful?"

Rav Nachman replied, "It was as painless as lifting a hair from a cup of milk. But were the Holy One, blessed be He, to say to me, 'You may return to that world where you were before,' I would not wish to do it. The fear of death is too great."

Mo'ed Katan 28a

155. Rav Sheshet noticed the Angel of Death in the marketplace. He said, "Do you want to take me here in the marketplace like an animal? Come home with me!"

Mo'ed Katan 28a

156. Rabbi Levi said:

"And David the King" is mentioned nearly fifty-two times. However, when he was dying, what is recorded is only this—"When David's life was drawing to a close. . . ."—indicating that no one wields power on the day of death.

I Kings 2:1
Ecclesiastes Rabba 8:11

157. Two good things are near to you and far from you, far from you and near to you:

Repentance is near to you and far from you, far from you and near to you.

Death is near to you and far from you, far from you and near to you.

Ecclesiastes Rabba 8:17

158. The rabbis said to Rav Hamnuna Zuti at the wedding of Mar the son of Ravina, "Please sing for us!"

He said, "Woe for us that we are to die! Woe for us that we are to die!"

They said to him, "What is our chorus?"

He said, "Where is the Torah and the Mitzvah that will protect us?"

Berachot 31a

159. Our rabbis have taught:

God decided to create three things, and even had He not decided to do so, it would have been only right for Him to consider them—
That corpses should decompose,
That the dead should be forgotten from the heart,
And that produce should rot with the passage of time.

Pesachim 54b

160. It is improper for someone to walk in a cemetery with his Tfillin on or carrying a Sefer Torah and reading from it. If he does so, he violates the negative Mitzvah of, "One who disparages the unfortunate, blasphemes his Creator." (Proverbs 17:5)

Berachot 18a

161. At the resurrection of the dead, the handicapped will arise still disabled, and then they will be cured.

Sanhedrin 91b

162. A certain non-Jew once asked Rabbi Yehoshua ben Korcha, "Do you not claim that the Holy One, blessed be He, sees into the future?"

"Yes, certainly," the rabbi replied.

The man said, "But it is written, 'And the Lord regretted that He had made people on earth, and His heart was saddened'"? (Genesis 6:6)

The rabbi asked, "Have you ever had a son?"

He replied, "Yes."

"And what did you do when he was born?"

He answered, "I was overjoyed and made everyone else joyous."

The rabbi asked, "And did you not know that some day the child would die?"

He answered, "At the time when one should be joyous—be joyous. And when it is time to mourn—mourn."

The rabbi said, "So, too, with the Holy One, blessed be He."

Genesis Rabba 27:7

163. Rabbi Yochanan said:

A person's feet are responsible for him. They will lead him to the place where he is wanted.

Sukkah 53a

164. Concerning the Future it is said,
"He will destroy death forever.
My Lord God will wipe away the tears from all faces." (Isaiah 25:8)

Mishna Mo'ed Katan 3:9

165. Our rabbis have taught:

A funeral procession must make way for a wedding procession.

Ketubot 17a

166. At first, burying the dead was more difficult for the relatives than the death itself—because of the enormous expense. Relatives even abandoned the bodies and ran away. Finally, Rabban Gamliel adopted a simple style, and the people carried him to his grave in linen garments. Subsequently everyone followed his example and carried out the dead in similar fashion—even in rough cloth worth only a Zuz.

Ketubot 8b

167. Rabbi Yannai said to his children:

My children, do not bury me either in white or black garments—white, because I may not be privileged, and I would be like a bridegroom among mourners,

and black, because I may be privileged, and I would be like a mourner among bridegrooms.

Rather bury me in the red garments that are imported from the sea provinces.

Shabbat 114a

168. It has been the custom in some places for a number of people to be buried in coffins which were made from the tables upon which they studied, or upon which they fed the poor, or upon which they worked faithfully at their trade.

Kav HaYashar, Chapter 46
(Kol Bo Al Avaylut, p. 182)

169. We need not make monuments for the righteous—their words serve as their memorial.

Shekalim 2:5

55

170. Comforters in a Shiva-house should not begin speaking until the mourner begins the conversation. The mourner sits in a central place, and once the mourner shakes his head to indicate that the comforters should leave, the comforters are no longer permitted to sit with him. (Neither a mourner nor a sick person is required to stand, even in the presence of the Nasi [the leader of the Jewish community].)

Shulchan Aruch,
Yoreh De'ah 376:1

171. Do not attempt to comfort a person whose dead relative still lies before him.

Pirke Avot 4:23

172. If someone who is not well sustains a loss, he should not be informed of it, to prevent him from becoming frantic.

Mo'ed Katan 26b

173. Simcha is forbidden to a mourner. Therefore, he should not pick up an infant, so that he will not begin to laugh.

Mo'ed Katan 26b

174. A person should not mourn too much for the deceased, and anyone who mourns too much, weeps [or: will weep] for someone else.

Rather, there should be three days for tears, seven days for lamenting, and thirty days to refrain from cutting the hair and wearing pressed clothes.

Shulchan Aruch,
Yoreh De'ah 394:1

175. Anyone who weeps and mourns for a worthy person shall have his sins forgiven because of the honor he has shown for that person.

Mo'ed Katan 25a

BOOK TWO

TABLE OF CONTENTS: Book Two

INTRODUCTION

This volume continues the work begun last year with the publication of my first anthology of Midrash and Halachah, *Where Heaven and Earth Touch*. That book has been successfully used for adult and teen-age seminars, classes, retreats, and study groups, and now I would like to offer more selections from our vast Rabbinic literature—making them available to those who wish to search yet further for Jewish values through the classical texts.

Once again, this is a rather personal selection. Some would say that a number of my choices are off the beaten track of normal study. That is true. But each is taken from the major works of our tradition, and, if they have been somewhat neglected in the regular course of study, perhaps now they will take a more substantial place in the everyday thinking of those who are exposed to them.

In this volume I struggled more with gender-translations, the he's and she's and himself's and herself's that would perhaps equalize certain imbalances in the implications of the subject matter. There are inconsistencies, and sometimes the end result became too cumbersome to accommodate a smoothness and evenness that would have been more pleasing to all. I leave the student to continue that particular struggle.

The single most important article on studying classical Jewish texts in translation is Arthur Kurzweil's "I Can't Read Much Hebrew, I Can't Read Much Aramaic, I Never Went to Yeshiva, But I Study Talmud Every Chance I Get" which first appeared in Moment Magazine a couple of years ago. It stands as *the* critical piece for anyone whose training in Semitic languages has been less-than-satisfactory, and should be read by anyone interested in pursuing the study of Jewish values material in English.*

Ultimately, my hope is that the student of these texts will, at moments, be swept away, staggered, touched by the sublimity and grandeur of Torah texts and their wisdom. The subject at hand is the broadest of all: Living Life with Meaning, The Human Touch. I would wish to engender a certain hunger in the reader, a craving to search ever deeper into the volumes upon volumes of our tradition—without being intimidated either by the quantity or the occasional difficulty of the words. This craving can be satisfied under the supervision of an appropriate, caring teacher, and in the presence of a *Chaver*, a friend with whom one can share the joy of Torah study. As I have been blessed with an abundance of such teachers and friends, so, too, do I wish the same for the readers of this volume.

Danny Siegel
April 10, 1984

*Kurzweil's article is available as a reprint through USY, c/o Jules Gutin, 155 5th Ave., New York, NY 10010

TORAH I: TORAH AND PEOPLE

1. Rabbi Yehoshua ben Levi said;

If you are alone on a journey, you should occupy yourself with Torah. . . .
If you have a headache, you should occupy yourself with Torah. . . .
If you have a sore throat, you should occupy yourself with Torah. . . .
If you have a pain in your bones, you should occupy yourself with
    Torah. . . .
If your entire body is in pain, you should occupy yourself with Torah. . . .

Eruvin 54a

2. Rabbi Simla'i sermonized:

The Torah begins and ends with acts of lovingkindness—
It begins with an act of lovingkindness, as it says,
"The Lord made clothing of skins for Adam and his wife, and he clothed
    them." (Genesis 3:20)
It ends with an act of lovingkindness, as it says,
"And He buried Moses there in the valley." (Deuteronomy 34:6)

Sotah 14a

3. All those years the Jews were in the desert, they carried two containers with
    them—
        one of the dead [containing the bones of Joseph],
        and one of the living [containing the Ten Commandments and the
            broken pieces of the first tablets]—
        and they were carried side-by-side.
Passers-by would ask, "What is the nature of these two containers?"
The Jews replied, "One is for the dead, and one is for the Intimate Presence
    of God."
"And what right does this dead individual have to be carried so closely to
    God's Intimate Presence?"
They said, "This one lived out all the words that were written in the other
    one."

Sotah 13a–b

HUMAN BEING

4. "There are many with me." (Psalm 55:19)
   And who are they?
   They are the angels who watch over people.
   Rabbi Yehoshua ben Levi said:
   An entourage of angels always walks in front of people,
        with messengers calling out.
   And what do they say?
   "Make way for the image of the Holy One, blessed be He!"

   Deuteronomy Rabba (Lieberman Edition), Re'eh 4

5. When the Jews left Egypt,
        almost all of them were disabled.
   How did that happen to be?
   They had been working with clay and bricks,
        climbing to the tops of buildings.
   Those doing the construction work
        would get to the upper levels of the building
        and a rock would fall on them
        and cut off their hands,
        or a beam
        or some clay would get into their eyes,
        blinding them.
   That is how they became disabled.

   Numbers Rabba, Naso 7:1

6a. One who sees

an Ethiopian

or a Gichor, i.e., one whose skin is extremely red,

or a Lavkan, i.e., an albino,

or a Kippayach, i.e., one whose stomach is inordinately large, and because of his wide girth his height seems shorter than it really is,*

or a dwarf,

or a Drakona, i.e., one who is covered with blemishes, . . .

or an elephant,

or a monkey,

recites the blessing,

"Blessed are You, O Lord, our God, Ruler of the universe, Who creates a variety of creations."

*Shulchan Aruch,
Orach Chaim, 225:8*

*Other interpret: one who is inordinately tall and thin.

6b. One who sees

a lame person,

or one without hands or legs,

or a blind person,

or one who has boils,

or a Bahakan, i.e., one who is pocked with small pockmarks,

if this has been their condition from birth,

we recite the blessing,

"Blessed are You, O Lord, our God, Ruler of the universe, Who creates a variety of creations."

But if these occurred after birth,

we recite the blessing,

"Blessed are You, O Lord, our God, Ruler of the universe, the True Judge."

There is an opinion that says this blessing is to be recited only if one is distressed about the person. . . .

The blessing is recited only the first time we see them,

when the strangeness of their appearance is most striking.

*Shulchan Aruch,
Orach Chaim, 225:9*

7. Rabbi Yochanan was sitting in front of the Babylonian Synagogue in Tzip-
   pori, reciting the Shema.
   When a prominent Roman official walked by, he did not rise in his honor.
   The official's aides were going to beat the rabbi, but he restrained them, saying,
   "Leave him alone. He is engrossed in the laws of his creator."

   Rabbi Chanina and Rabbi Yehoshua ben Levi once went to the Roman pro-
   consul in Caesarea.
   As soon as he saw them, he arose.
   The others who were present said,
   "Why do you rise before those Jews?"
   He said to them,
   "I see in their faces the faces of angels."

   Jerusalem Talmud,
   Berachot 5:1

8. Issi ben Yehuda says:

   "You shall rise before the aged" (Leviticus 19:32) applies to all aged people.
   Rabbi Yochanan said:
   The law is according to Issi ben Yehuda.
   Rabbi Yochanan used to rise in the presence of aged non-Jews, saying, "How
       many experiences have happened to these people!"
   . . . .
   Abbaye would give his hand to the elderly.

   Kiddushin 33|a

9. With tears in his eyes, Rabbi Yehuda the Prince said:
   There are those who acquire eternity after many years,
       and others who achieve the same in a single moment.

   Avoda Zara 18a

MONEY I: TZEDAKAH

10. If you have done the Mitzvah of Tzedakah,
    you will be privileged to be wealthy.
And if you are privileged to be wealthy,
    do the Mitzvah of Tzedakah with your wealth.

Derech Eretz Zuta 4

11. It was said of Rabbi Tarfon
    that he was very wealthy
    but did not give (sufficient)* Tzedakah–money to the poor.
Rabbi Akiva once found him and said:
    My teacher,
    would you like me to purchase a city or two for you?
Rabbi Tarfon replied:
    Yes.
And he immediately gave him four thousand gold dinars.
Rabbi Akiva took the money
    and distributed it to the poor.
A while later,
Rabbi Tarfon found him and said:
    Where are the cities you purchased for me?
He took him by the hand
    and brought him to the house of Torah-study.
    He then took a copy of the Book of Psalms
    and placed it in front of them.
They read and read,
    until they came to the verse,
    "If a person gives freely to the poor,
    his Tzedakah-acts will stand him in good stead forever." (Psalm 112:9)
Rabbi Akiva said to him:
    This is the city I bought for you!
Rabbi Tarfon arose
    and kissed him on the head
    and said:
    My teacher, my hero!
    My teacher in wisdom!
    My hero in the essences of Life!
He then gave him more money to give away.

Massechet Kallah,
Towards the end

*The Gaon of Vilna adds the word "sufficient" to the text.

12. It is good to give to Tzedakah before praying.

Shulchan Aruch,
Orach Chaim 92:10

13. We have never seen—nor have we ever heard of—a Jewish community
that does not have a weekly food distribution for the poor.
As for a daily food distribution—
some places have it, and some do not.
Nowadays, the prevailing custom is this:
The collectors make the rounds every day and distribute the food
every Friday.

Maimonides, Mishna Torah,
Laws of Gifts to the Poor 9:3

14. Rabbi Yossi said:

I would rather be a Tzedakah-collector than a Tzedakah-distributor.

Shabbat 118b

15. Rabbi Yochanan said:

All the prophets were wealthy.

Nedarim 38a

16. Rabbi Yochanan said:

The Holy One, blessed be He, allows His Intimate Presence to be felt only by
those who are strong, wealthy, wise, and humble.

Nedarim 38a

17. Rabbi Yochanan said:

Rain is withheld only because of those who promise to give to Tzedakah but
do not fulfill their pledges, as the Biblical verse states,
"Clouds, wind—but no rain—
because of those who praise themselves about false gifts."
(Proverbs 25:14)

Ta'anit 8b,

18. Because you held your hands back from stealing—
what could evil people possibly do to you?
Because you did not close up your hand into a fist—
keeping yourself from doing Tzedakah—
what could people loaded with silver and gold possibly do to you?
Because your feet did not rush you to commit sins—
what could the Angel of Death possibly do to you?
These words of Mine are a warning:
Do what you wish,
but do not say,
"Nobody ever warned me."

Derech Eretz Zuta 4

19. One who gives to his grown sons and daughters—
even though he is not required to support them—
so that the sons may learn Torah
and the daughters may be guided in Menschlich living,
and similarly,
one who gives gifts to his parent—
all of these people being in need of this support—
these acts fall into the category of Tzedakah.
Not only that,
but these people take precedence over others.

Shulchan Aruch,
Yoreh De'ah 251:3

20. What is considered appropriate respect a child should have for a parent?
Feeding, giving to drink, clothing, covering, leading in and out
—doing all these things kindly—
for even if a child feeds a parent the finest delicacies every day,
but does it angrily,
he will be punished for it.

Shulchan Aruch,
Yoreh De'ah 240:4

21. The cost of the food and drink is to come from the parent's money,
    if the parent can afford it.
  But if the parent cannot afford it,
    and the child can,
    the child may be forced to feed the parent
    from whatever the child can afford.
  If, however, the child does not have the resources,
    the child is not required to go begging from door to door
    in order to feed the parent.
  Gloss: Some authorities rule that a child is not required to give
    more than what is in the child's Tzedakah-budget.
  In any event,
    if the child can afford it,
    a curse deserves to come upon a child
    who supports a parent from Tzedakah-money.
  And if there are many children,
    an accounting of their money is made,
    and if some of them are rich,
    and others poor,
    we obligate only the rich ones to support the parent.

Shulchan Aruch,
Yoreh De'ah 240:5,
With Isserles

22. We do not assign a specific sum to be collected from orphans—
    even for [the great Mitzvah of] Redeeming Captives—
    even if they have considerable money.
  This is the exception:
    we may assign a sum to be collected if it is for their own
    self-respect,
    so that, as a result, they will thereby acquire a fine reputation.

Shulchan Aruch,
Yoreh De'ah 248:3

23. The people of Alexandria asked Rabbi Yehoshua ben Chanania a dozen
   questions.
[One of them was:]
"What should a person do to acquire wisdom?"
He said to them,
"That person should sit long hours and study Torah,
   and engage in a minimum of business activities."
They said,
"But isn't it so that many have done the same,
   but have not succeeded?"
"Rather, let that person pray for a gracious gesture
   from The One Who is The Source of All Wisdom,
   as the verse states,
'For the Lord gives wisdom,
By His decrees, knowledge and insight come.'" (Proverbs 2:6)

[One of the other questions was:]
"What should a person do to become wealthy?"
He said to them,
"That person (should become very involved in business,
   but)* must be certain to conduct the business he does
   honestly and in good faith."
They said,
"But isn't it so that many have done the same,
   but have not succeeded?"
"Rather, let that person pray for a gracious gesture
   from The One Who is The Source of All Wealth,
   as the verse states,
'The silver is Mine,
   and the gold is Mine—
   says the Lord of Hosts.'" (Chaggai 2:8)

Niddah 69b, 70b

*The Gaon of Vilna omits this phrase from the text.

24. The Saintly Abba Tachna was once entering his city on Friday afternoon
near dusk with a bundle on his shoulder.
He came across a man suffering from boils lying at the crossroads.

The man said to him:

Rabbi, do an act of Tzedakah with me and take me into the city.

Abba Tachna said:

If I leave my package behind, how will my family and I support ourselves?
And if I leave this man who is suffering with boils, my life will be worthless.
What did he do?
He allowed his positive instincts to overcome his negative ones and brought
the suffering man into the city.
He then went back, picked up his bundle, and returned to the city just as the
sun was setting.
Everyone was astounded, saying:
Is this The Saintly Abba Tachna?*
Deeply troubled, he said:
Do you feel that I have, perhaps, desecrated the Shabbat?
At that moment, the Holy One, Blessed be He, made the sun shine,
as the Biblical verse says,
"A sun for Tzedakah shall rise for those who stand in awe of My name."
(Malachi 3:20)

Ecclesiastes Rabba 9:7

*The act of carrying an object from one domain to another is prohibited on Shabbat.

25. Even a poor person who is kept alive by Tzedakah funds must give Tzedakah
from what he receives.

Shulchan Aruch,
Yoreh De'ah 248:1

26. Two poor people—who are required to give Tzedakah—may exchange their
Tzedakah money with each other.

Shulchan Aruch,
Yoreh De'ah 251:12

27. It is customary to make Kiddush in the synagogue. . . .

This practice was established originally for the benefit of travellers who ate and drank in the synagogue so that they, too, could fulfill their Mitzvah-obligation.

This regulation is still in practice nowadays, even though travellers no longer eat in the synagogue.

Shulchan Aruch,
Orach Chaim 269:1

28. Even someone essentially supported by others—

if he has a little money of his own—

must push himself [to provide the things necessary] to honor the Shabbat. . . .

Therefore, he should limit his weekday expenses
in order to have enough to honor Shabbat.

Shulchan Aruch,
Orach Chaim 242:1

29a. Even if a person has nothing to eat, he should go begging door-to-door in order to get oil for a Shabbat light, as the light is considered in the category of "Shabbat Delight."

Shulchan Aruch,
Orach Chaim 263:2

29b. *The meaning of this passage is not that he has nothing to eat at all—because then it would be better for him to beg in order to buy bread.*

With bread he can perform the Mitzvah of Kiddush and also the minimum requirement for a Shabbat meal.

Rather, the meaning is:

he does not have enough money of his own to purchase Shabbat food, but instead receives from the community Tzedakah fund.

Even in that case he must also try to obtain a light for Shabbat.

Mishna Berura 9 to
Shulchan Aruch,
Orach Chaim 263:2

30. If a person cannot afford both oil for the Chanukkah Menorah and for wine for Havdalah, the Chanukkah light takes precedence.

Shulchan Aruch,
Orach Chaim 296:5

31. Even a poor person who is fed from Tzedakah funds should sell his clothing, or borrow, or hire himself out in order to have four cups of wine on Passover.

Shulchan Aruch,
Orach Chaim 472:13

32. [The communal Tzedakah administrators] must give a person at least four cups of wine [for Passover], even [if he is so poor that he eats regularly] from the local soup kitchen.

Pesachim 99b

33. We are required to provide for the poor on Purim day.
The minimum is to provide for two poor people—
    giving to each one a gift, or money, or cooked food, or other kinds of
    food,
    as the verse states,
    ". . . and presents to the poor" [plural] (Esther 9:22)-
    two presents to two poor people.
Furthermore, we should not be too meticulous concerning Purim Tzedakah-
    money: anyone who puts out his hand to take—should be given money.
Money set aside for Purim-money in the community Tzedakah fund must not
    be used for any other purpose.

It is better for people to spend more on gifts to the poor for Purim
    than to spend more for their own Purim meal
    or for sending packets of goodies to their friends [Mishloach Manot],
    for there is no greater or more glorious joy
    than to bring happiness
    to the hearts of the poor, orphans, widows, and strangers.
One who brings joy to the hearts of these disadvantaged individuals resembles
    God,
    as the verse states,

"[For thus says The One Who lives forever in the most sublime heights,
whose name is holy:
I live on high, in holiness;
Yet I am with the contrite and downtrodden—]
reviving the spirits of the lowly,
reviving the hearts of the disadvantaged." (Isaiah 57:15)

Maimonides, Mishnah Torah
Laws of Megillah, 2:16-17

TORAH II: SAGES AND STUDENTS

34. Rava said:

> If you see a student whose Torah-study is as hard as iron to him,
>   the reason must be that the teacher was not gentle enough with him. . .
> How may the situation be corrected?
> Let the student surround himself with many good friends.

Ta'anit 8a

35. Rabbi Yossi says:

> Anyone who teaches Torah in public and does not make the words
>   as pleasant as honey from the honeycomb for those who are listening—
> it were better that he not teach the words at all.

The Rabbis said:

> Anyone who teaches Torah in public and does not make the words
>   as pleasant to those who are listening as honey and milk mixed together—
> it were better that he not teach the words at all.

Song of Songs Rabba 4:11, 1

36. Rabbi Yochanan said:

> If the teacher resembles an angel of God, seek Torah from him,
>   but if not, do not seek Torah from him.

Mo'ed Katan 17a
[see Malachi 2:7]

37. Rabbi Meir says:

> If you have studied with one teacher, do not say, "It is enough,"
>   but, rather, go study with another, too.
> However, don't go to study with just anybody;
>   go to someone who is essentially close to you,
>   because the verse in Proverbs says (5:15),
> "Drink water from your own cistern,
>   running water from your own well."

Avot DeRabbi Natan A:3

38. Rava said:

> See how foolish people are—
>   they rise before a Torah scroll,
>   but do not rise in the presence of a great person!

39. The question was posed:

> Should people rise before a Torah scroll?

> Rabbi Chilkia, Rabbi Simon, and Rabbi Elazar all say:

> Simple logic dictates that they should—
> If we rise before those who are students of Torah,
>   how much more so should we rise before the Torah itself!

Kiddushin 33b

40. Rabbi Elazar said:

> Any sage who does not rise in the presence of his or her Masterteacher is
>   considered wicked,
>   and will not live long,
>   and will forget the Torah he or she has learned.

Kiddushin 33b

41a. An animal's carcass is better than a sage who doesn't abide by the rules of
common decency.

Leviticus Rabba 1:15
(1st Translation)

41b. An animal's carcass is better than a sage who doesn't have common sense.

Leviticus Rabba 1:15
(2nd Translation)

42a. An animal is better than a sage without sensitivity to people's feelings.

Seder Eliahu Rabba (6) 7,
Friedmann, p. 33
(1st Translation)

42b. An animal is better than a sage who doesn't know how to treat others decently.

Seder Eliahu Rabba (6) 7,
Friedmann, p. 33
(2nd Translation)

43a. Rabbi Akiva said:

To what can we compare someone who is arrogant because of his Torah-study?
To an animal's carcass thrown by the side of the road. Everyone who passes
by puts his hand on his nose, stays far away, and goes on as quickly as possible.

Avot DeRabbi Natan A: 11
(1st Translation)

43b. Rabbi Akiva said:

What is a person like who sets himself above the words of Torah?
Like an animal's carcass thrown by the side of the road. Everyone who walks
by puts his hand on his nose, keeps his distance, then moves on.

Avot DeRabbi Natan A: 11
(2nd Translation)

44. "A person who separates himself destroys the world." (Proverbs 29:4)—

This refers to a sage
    who knows the laws,
    their interpretations and derivations,
    and substantive and ethical tales,
    but, when a widow and orphan come to him to decide their case,
    he says,
    "I am busy with my Torah-study.
    I have no free time."

The Lord says to him,
    "I consider this as though you have destroyed the world."

That is the meaning of the verse,
    "A person who separates himself, destroys the world."

Exodus Rabba 30:13

45. A person should ask about the meaning of a verse or a law —even if everyone will laugh at him.

Seder Eliahu Rabba 13:6

46a. Rabbi Chiyya bar Nechemia said:

If a student does not consider it necessary to quote a selection of Torah in the name of his teacher, his Torah will be forgotten.
It is for this reason that the teacher must impress himself on the student.

Ecclesiastes Rabba 2:15, 5
(First Translation)

46b. Rabbi Chiyya bar Nechemia said:

If a student does not consider it necessary to quote a selection of Torah in the name of his teacher, his Torah will be forgotten.
It is for this reason that the teacher must apply himself intensively with the student.

Ecclesiastes Rabba 2:15, 5
(Second Translation)

47. Did not Rabbi Yochanan once say:

Rabbi Oshaya BeRibi had a dozen students,
    and I spent eighteen days among them.
I studied the heart of every single one of them,
    and the wisdom of every single one.

Eruvin 53a

48. Avtalyon says:

Sages!
Be careful with your words!
You may be punished with exile to a place where the water is harmful,
    and the students who follow you will die,
    and, as a result, the Name of Heaven will be desecrated.

Sayings of the Fathers 1:11

49. Issi ben Yehuda says:

Why do sages die before their time?
Not because they are adulterers or thieves,
    but because they do not take care of themselves.

Avot DeRabbi Natan A: 29

50. Our Rabbis have taught:

Three kinds of people hate each other—
    dogs, chickens, and Persian sorcerers.
There are those who add prostitutes to the list.
And there are those who add Babylonian sages to the list.

Pesachim 113b

51. Rabban Yochanan ben Zakkai had five students.
As long as he was alive, they stayed near him and studied Torah in his presence.
When he died, they all went to Yavneh, except Rabbi Elazar ben Arach who
    went to Emmaus, where his wife was.
It was a place of refreshing waters and wonderful climate.
He waited for the others to come to him, but they did not come.
When he saw that they would not come to him, he wanted to go to them,
    but his wife would not let him.

She said:

Who needs whom?

He said:

They need me.

She said to him:

In the case of a container of food and mice, who goes to whom?
Do the mice come to the container of food—
    or does the container go to the mice?
He listened to her and stayed where he was, until he forgot his knowledge of
    Torah.
A while later, they came to him and asked him a legal question,
    but he did not know how to answer them.

Ecclesiastes Rabbi 7:7, 2

52. "And raise many students" (Pirke Avot 1:1)—

The School of Shammai says:

A person should teach only those who are wise, humble, a descendant of distinguished people, and wealthy.

The School of Hillel says:

A person should teach everyone, for there were many Jewish sinners who became attached to Torah study, and, as a result, righteous, pious, and decent people came from them.

Avot DeRabbi Natan A: 3

53. Hillel the Elder had eighty students.
Thirty of them were worthy of having God's Intimate Presence rest on them as it did on Moshe, our Teacher—but their generation was not worthy of this.
Thirty of them were worthy of having the sun stand still for them as it did for Joshua ben Nun.
And twenty of them had moderate talents.
The greatest of them all was Yonatan ben Uzziel.
The least of them all was Rabban Yochanan ben Zakkai.

Bava Batra 134a and
Avot DeRabbi Natan A:14

54. Among the greatest sages of Israel were woodcutters, waterdrawers, and blind people.
Nevertheless, they were involved in Torah study day and night.

Maimonides, Mishneh Torah,
Laws of Torah Study 1:9

55. Just as a person is required to teach his child,
so, too, is he required to teach his grandchild,
as the verse states,
"And make these things known to your children and to your grandchildren."
(Deuteronomy 4:9)

Maimonides, Mishneh Torah,
Laws of Torah Study 1:2

56. Issi ben Yehuda used to characterize the unique qualities of the sages in the following manner:

Rabbi Meir—a sage and a scribe.
Rabbi Yehuda—wise when he wanted to be.
Rabbi Tarfon—a pile of nuts.
Rabbi Yishmael—a fully-stocked store.
Rabbi Akiva—a bursting treasure.
Rabbi Yochanan ben Nuri—a peddler's basket.
Rabbi Elazar ben Azariah—a basket of spices.
Rabbi Eliezer ben Ya'acov's Mishna is limited in quantity but fine quality.
Rabbi Yossi—his reasoning is always sound.
Rabbi Shimon would grind great quantities but produce only a little.
This was explained to mean that he forgot only a little, and what he disposed
of was only the bran.

Gittin 67a

57. David made this request:

"O may I live in Your tent, [O God,] forever." (Psalm 61:5)
Did David really think that he would live forever?
The meaning is this—
David said,
"May I privileged to have my words quoted in my name in the synagogues
and houses of Torah study."

Jerusalem Talmud,
Berachot 2:1

MY FAVORITE RABBI: CHANINA BEN DOSA

58. Once upon a time,
> while Rabbi Chanina ben Dosa was out walking,
> it began to rain.

He said:

Master of the Universe!
The entire world is comfortable,
> and Chanina has to suffer?
The rain stopped.

When he got back to his house,
he said:
Master of the Universe!
The entire world is suffering,
> and Chanina is comfortable?
And the rain began to fall again.

Ta'anit 24b

59. Once upon a time,
Rabbi Chanina ben Dosa saw the people of his town taking a variety of offerings and gifts up to Jerusalem.

He said:

Everyone is taking gifts and offerings up to Jerusalem,
> and I am taking nothing.
What did he do?
He went to the outskirts of town and found a fine stone which he cut, and shaped, and polished,

and then he said:

I hereby promise to take this up to Jerusalem.
When he tried to find workers to carry it, five people appeared.

He asked:

Will you take this stone up to Jerusalem?

They said:

Give us fifty * coins, and we will take it up to Jerusalem.
He wanted to give them the money, but discovered that he did not have any
    money at the time.
So the workers went away.
The Holy One, blessed be He, then arranged for five angels in the form of
    people to appear to him.

He said to them:

Will you take this stone up for me?

They said:

Give us five coins, and we will take your stone up to Jerusalem, on the condi-
    tion that you, too, help with the carrying.
He placed his hands on the stone and wrapped his fingers around it, and sud-
    denly they found themselves standing in Jerusalem.
When he wanted to pay the workers, he could not find them.
He went into the Chamber of Cut Stone in the Temple,
    where the Sanhedrin held its sessions, and asked about them.
The members of the Sanhedrin said:

It appears that angels brought your stone up to Jerusalem.

Ecclesiastes Rabba 1:1, 1

*Other texts read, "five."

TORAH III: TORAH

60. Rava said:

A person should always study texts,
  even though he may forget,
  even though he may not understand what he is reciting.

Avoda Zara 19a

61. It is a positive commandment for every Jew to write a Sefer Torah. Even if his parents left him a Sefer Torah, it is a Mitzvah for him to write one for himself.

Shulchan Aruch,
Yoreh De'ah 270:1

62. Rabbi Abbahu said:

The verse . . . "It is difficult work that God has given to people to be involved in" (Ecclesiastes 1:13)
  refers to the way Torah-study works—
  people study it and they forget it.

The Babylonian Rabbis said in the name of Rabbi Yitzchak from Israel, and Rabbi Tuviah said in the name of Rabbi Yitzchak:

It is beneficial for them to study and then forget,
  for if they studied and did not forget,
  they would spend only two or three years involved in Torah-study,
  and then go back to their jobs.
  Then they would never again pay attention to Torah.
  But since people study Torah and forget it,
  they never lose contact with words of Torah.

Ecclesiastes Rabba 1:13

63. Rabbi Abbahu came to Tiberias.

When Rabbi Yochanan's students saw that Rabbi Abbahu's face was glowing,
  they said to Rabbi Yochanan,
"Rabbi Abbahu must have found some treasure!"
He said to them,
  "And why is that?"
They said,
  "Because his face is glowing."
He said to them,
  "Perhaps he has heard a new insight into Torah."
Rabbi Yochanan then went to Rabbi Abbahu and said,
  "What new Torah-idea did you hear?"
He said to him,
  "I discovered something in an ancient selection from the Tosefta that I
  had never seen before."
Rabbi Yochanan then applied this verse to him,
  "Human wisdom makes the face glow." (Ecclesiastes 8:1)

Jerusalem Talmud,
Pesachim 10:1

64. Rabbi Eliezer had a student who used to study silently, and after three years
he forgot what he had learned.

Eruvin 54a

65. Rabbi Elazar said:

Whoever makes himself forget any of his Torah-knowledge will cause his
children to go into exile.

Yoma 38b

66. Rabbi Yochanan said:

The Holy One, blessed be He, gives wisdom only to those who are already
  wise, as the verse says,
"He gives wisdom to the wise,
  and knowledge to those who have insight." (Daniel 2:21)

Berachot 55a

67. Rabbi Yossi ben Kisma said:

I was once walking along
when a man came up to me and said,
"Shalom."

I answered,
"Shalom."

He said to me,
"Rabbi, where are you from?"

I said,
"I am from a great city of sages and scholars."

He said to me,
"Rabbi, would you like to live with us, in our place?
I will give you a million gold dinars, and jewels, and pearls."

I said to him,
"Even if you were to give me all the silver and gold and jewels and pearls
in the world,
I would not live anywhere but a place of Torah.
That is what is written in the Book of Psalms,
composed by David, King of Israel,
'I prefer the Torah You teach—
more than thousands of gold and silver pieces.' (Psalm 119:72)
Not only that,
but when a person dies,
silver and gold and jewels and pearls do not accompany that person.
Only his Torah-knowledge and his good deeds go with him,
as the verse says,
'When you walk, it will guide you;
When you lie down, it will watch over you;
And when you awaken, it will talk with you.' (Proverbs 6:22)
'When you walk, it will guide you'—in this world;
'When you lie down, it will watch over you'—in the grave;
'And when you awaken, it will talk with you'—in the Future World.
Furthermore, another verse says,
'Silver is Mine, and gold is Mine—says the Lord of Hosts.' " (Chaggai 2:8)

Sayings of the Fathers 6:9

68. [Because you would not serve the Lord your God in joy and gladness over the abundance of everything, you shall have to serve the enemies the Lord will send against you in hunger and thirst, naked,] and lacking everything (Deuteronomy 28:47–48)—

Rabbi Ammi said in the name of Rav:

"Lacking everything" means you will be without a candle and a table.

Rav Chisda said:

Without a spouse.

Rav Sheshet said:

Without a servant.

Rav Nachman said:

Without knowledge.

A Tanna taught:

Without salt and without fat.

Abbaye said:

We have a tradition that says that true poverty is poverty of the mind.

In Israel there is a saying:
Whoever has this, has everything.
Whoever does not have this, what does he have?
Whoever acquires this, what does he lack?
Whoever has not acquired this, what does he own?

Nedarim 41a

69a. Mari bar Rav Huna said:

People should say good-bye with a word of Torah-law, because that way he will remember him.

Eruvin 64a
(First Translation)

69b. Mari bar Rav Huna said:

People should say good-bye with a word of Torah-law, because that way he will remember it.

Eruvin 64a
(Second Translation)

88

70. People should say good-bye not with chatter, nor with senseless joking, nor with inanities, nor with meaningless words, but rather with a word of Torah.

Jerusalem Talmud,
Berachot 5:1

71. People should say good-bye not with chatter, nor with senseless joking, nor with inanities, but rather with words of wisdom.

Tosefta Berachot,
Lieberman 3:21

72. Transgression extinguishes the light radiated by Mitzvot, but it does not extinguish the light of Torah.

Sotah 21a

73. Rabbi Abbahu said in the name of Rabbi Yochanan:

When the Holy One, blessed be He, gave the Torah—no bird chirped, nor was the sound of fluttering wings to be heard.
Oxen did not bellow, angels did not fly, nor did the Serafim-angels chant, "Holy, Holy Holy."
The sea did not stir.
Not a single creature spoke.
Rather, the entire world was still.
Then—and only then—was the sound heard,
"Anochi . . . I am the Lord, your God." (Exodus 20:2)

Exodus Rabba 29:9

74. Rabbi Akiva was once giving a Torah-lecture, but the assembled crowd was falling asleep.
He wanted to wake them up, so he said:

How is it that Esther came to rule over 127 provinces?
It makes sense—Esther, the descendant of Sarah, who lived 127 years, by rights should rule over 127 provinces.

Genesis Rabba 58:1

75. Whoever thinks that he should study Torah and not work, but rather be supported by Tzedakah, desecrates God's name, debases the Torah, and extinguishes the light of our religion.

He also causes injury to himself and denies himself a place in the Future World, because it is forbidden to derive benefit from the study of Torah.

Maimonides, Mishneh Torah,
Laws of Torah Study 3:10

76. A person should not say,

"I will study the Written Torah so I will be called 'Sage,' "

"I will study the Oral Torah so that I will be called 'Rabbi,' "

"I will study the Oral Torah so that I will become an Elder, sitting among the other Elders."

Rather, study out of a sense of love, and eventually the honor will come of its own.

Nedarim 62a

77. *There is no prohibition against calling one who is Torah-ignorant to the Torah before a Torah-sage, if he is a distinguished person for other reasons, and wealthy, and a leader of the generation.*

This is not considered disrespect to the Torah-sage. On the contrary, it is considered a sign of respect to the Torah, because it is being honored by great people.

Gloss by Isserles to Shulchan Aruch,
Orach Chaim 282:3

(*A possible alternate translation might read, "if he is a distinguished person for other reasons, or wealthy, or a leader of the generation.")

MONEY II: MONEY

78. The arcade of city accountants' offices was outside the city limits of Jerusalem.
Whoever wanted to review his accounts would go there.
Why [were the accountants' offices outside of the city]?
In case a person would become depressed when reviewing his accounts—and
Jerusalem was to be known as "The joy of the entire earth." (Psalm 48:3)

Exodus Rabba, End of Pekuday

79. Rava said:

People become poor for three reasons—
because they free their pagan slaves,
and because they inspect their property on Shabbat,
and because they fix their main meal on Shabbat during the time when
Torah is being taught in the House of Study.

Gittin 38b

80. Solomon said,

"Who has eaten as I have eaten?
Who has drunk as I have drunk?
And who has done what I have done?"

Rabbi Yirmiah said in the name of Rabbi Shmuel bar Rav Yitzchak:

Solomon had a giant eagle upon which he rode back and forth as far as
Palmyra in the wilderness—reaching Palmyra and returning in one day.

Ecclesiastes Rabba 2:25

81a. There once was a certain glutton who worked six days a week throughout
the year but had nothing to eat on Shabbat.
What did he do?
He put on his best clothes, jumped off the roof, and died.

Ecclesiastes Rabba 2:16
(First Translation)

81b. There once was a certain glutton who worked six days a week throughout
the year but had nothing to eat on Shabbat.
What did he do?
He put on his work clothes, jumped off the roof, and died.

Ecclesiastes Rabba 2:16
(Second Translation)

82. Rabbi Yehoshua ben Levi said:

Whoever accepts the hospitality of a stingy person transgresses a negative
    Mitzvah, as the verses explain,
"Do not eat of a stingy man's food;
Do not have a craving for his delicacies;
He is like one who keeps accounts;
He says to you, 'Eat and drink,'
But he does not really mean it.
You will vomit up the little bit you ate,
And you will waste your pleasant words." (Proverbs 23:6–8)

Sotah 38b

83. There once was a man who accumulated a supply of wine and oil, but he
    would not give the appropriate tithes.
What did the Holy One, blessed be He, do?
He put into him a demonic spirit of madness.
The man took a club and began smashing the barrels of wine and oil.
One member of the household began to shout at him.
What did the man do?
He took the club and beat the other on the head, saying:
I curse you because you won't help me.
The other said:
Give me a club, and I will also smash the barrels.
While one smashed one barrel, the other would smash two of them..
And what was the cause of all of this?
The fact that he did not give the appropriate tithes.

Tanchuma, Buber
Re'eh, 9

84. There once was a certain man who was known as, "The Mouse Who Sits on
His Dinars."

Sanhedrin 29b

85. It's not the mouse that's the thief—it's the hole."

Kiddushin 56b

86. "One who shares with a thief is his own enemy. . . ." (Proverbs 29:24)

It once happened that a certain Roman governor would kill those who
   bought stolen goods and would let the thieves go.
Everyone ridiculed him, saying he wasn't handling the matter properly.
What did the governor do?
He issued a proclamation in his province—
"Everyone to the playing field!"
What did he do?
He brought weasels and put food in front of them.
The weasels took the food and put them in their holes.
The next day the governor issued another proclamation, saying,
"Everyone to the playing field!"
What did he do?
He brought the weasels, put food in front of them, but plugged up their holes.
When the weasels took the food and brought them to their holes, they found
   them plugged.
So they brought the food back to where they had gotten it.
Does this not indicate that everything in the cycle results from those who
   purchase the stolen goods?

Yalkut Shimoni,
Proverbs 962

87. "I have seen an evil done under the sun." (Ecclesiastes 6:1)

Rabbi Shmuel bar Ammi said:

This refers to the tricks of dishonest merchants—
   the ones who adulterate wine with water,
   oil with poppy juice, honey with wild strawberry juice,
   . . . and to those who use a cross-bar on their scales that is longer on one
   side than on the other.

Ecclesiastes Rabba 6:1, 1

88. Rabbi Levi said:

The punishments for having false measures in business are more harsh than
for sexual improprieties with forbidden relatives [Leviticus 18].

Yevamot 21a

89. Rabbi Levi said:

Robbing human beings is worse than robbing objects that belong to God.

Bava Batra 88b

90. When a poor person would come to Sodom, everyone would give him a coin
upon which was written the giver's name.
But they wouldn't sell the poor person any bread.
When the poor person died, each came and re-claimed his coin.

Sanhedrin 109b

91. There was a young woman in Sodom who used to sneak bread to the poor in
a pitcher.
When the people of Sodom found out, they smeared her with honey and laid
her out on the city walls.
Wasps came and ate her.

Sanhedrin 109b

92. Rava explained:

. . . .
With greed in their eyes, the people of Sodom would keep on the look-out for
wealthy people.
When they would find a rich person, they would have him sit near a pre-
cariously leaning wall.
Then they would push the wall on him and take his money.

Sanhedrin 109a

SHORTER SELECTIONS

93. The sages have said:

Stay away from hideous things
   and even things that appear to be hideous.

Chullin 44b

94. Our Rabbis have taught:

This is the way you should act towards people—
   though sometimes you may push them away with your left hand,
   draw them closer with your right.

Sanhedrin 107b

95. Rav Yehuda said in the name of Rav:
[In moral and ethical matters] you should never intentionally test yourself.

Sanhedrin 107a

96. The eye is shown only what it is capable of seeing,
   and the ear is given to hear only what it is capable of hearing.

Avot DeRabbi Natan A:2

97. The sages have said:

. . . .

Run to do a minor Mitzvah because it will bring you to major ones.

Avot DeRabbi Natan A:2

98. Everyone is required to recite at least one hundred blessings a day.

*Shulchan Aruch,
Orach Chaim 46:3*

99. You can always tell whether a person is a sage or an uncultured person by his blessings.

Jerusalem Talmud
Berachot 1:5

By the cigars they smoke and the composers they love ye shall know the texture of men's souls. (John Galsworthy)

100. Three things weaken a person.
These they are:
Anxiety,
travel,
and sin.

Gittin 70a

101. Three things are of equal importance:
wisdom,
fear of God,
and humility.

Derech Eretz Rabba 7

102. Ben Azzai used to say:

Come down two or three steps from your place and sit.
It is better for people to say to you, "Go up!" than for them to say, "Go down!"

Avot DeRabbi Natan A:25

103. The son of a king is a commoner.

Sanhedrin 18b

104. There are those who say that garlic brings in love and drives out jealousy.

Bava Kamma 82a

105. When the wine goes in, the secrets go out.

Eruvin 65a

106. A handful of food does not satisfy a lion.

Sanhedrin 16a

107. Rabbi Yehoshua ben Levi said:

A popular saying goes—
If one has been bitten by a snake, even a rope terrifies him.

Ecclesiastes Rabba 7:1, 4

108a. Whoever finds nothing but faults in others is himself full of faults, never finding anything good to say about anyone.

Derech Eretz Rabba 1
(First Translation)

108b. Whoever finds nothing but faults in others is himself defective, never saying anything good about the world.

Derech Eretz Rabba 1
(Second Translation)

108c. Whoever finds nothing but faults in others is himself defective; he never says anything good about anything in life.

Derech Eretz Rabba 1
(Third Translation)

108d. Whoever is unfit is always finding others unfit, and never has anything good to say about anyone.

Derech Eretz Rabba 1
(According to Vilna Gaon)

109. There can be famine for seven years, but it won't come to the gate of a craftsperson.

Sanhedrin 29a

110. Most Jews living in the Diaspora have non-Jewish names.

Gittin 11b

111. Rav Chisda said:

I prefer daughters to sons.

Bava Batra 141a

112. Rav Chiya bar Ashi said in the name of Rav:

The sages will not have rest even in the Future World.

Mo'ed Katan 29a

113. Whoever mourns for Jerusalem will be privileged to see her joyous times.

Ta'anit 30b

114. Resh Lakish said:

If the Garden of Eden is in Israel, the door to the Garden is in Bet She'an.

Eruvin 19a

115. It is forbidden to be involved with demons. There is one opinion, however, that permits asking them about stolen items.

Shulchan Aruch,
Yoreh De'ah 179:16

116. People should not get married except at the time of the month as the moon grows larger.

Shulchan Aruch,
Yoreh De'ah 179:2

THREE LONGER, UNUSUAL SELECTIONS

117. When did the Holy One, blessed be He, cause the population of Israelites
　　　to grow so dramatically in Egypt,
　　　as the verse would indicate,
　　　"I let you grow like the plants of the field,
　　　and you continued to grow . . ."? (Ezekiel 16:7)
Exactly how did this happen?
When Pharaoh decreed,
　　　"Every male child shall be thrown into the Nile," (Exodus 1:21)
　　　what did the Israelite women do?
When a woman would sense that she was beginning to go into labor,
　　　she would go into the field to have the child.
Once the child was born,
　　　the mother would turn her eyes to heaven and say,
　　　"I have done my part,
　　　just as You as told me—
　　　'Be fruitful and multiply.'—
　　　Now You do Your part!"
And what did the Egyptians do?
When the Egyptians saw the Israelite women
　　　going into the fields to have their children.
　　　they would sit opposite them,
　　　at a distance.
When the women would finish delivering the children,
　　　and would return to the city,
　　　the Egyptians then took stones
　　　and went to kill the babies.
The babies would be swallowed up in the field,
　　　and then reappear at a distance,
　　　and again be swallowed up,
　　　and again reappear at a distance.
Finally, the Egyptians became weary of this
　　　and went away.

And how did the babies survive out in the fields?
Rabbi Levi said:

The Holy One, blessed be He,
　　　would assign two angels to each baby,
　　　one to wash the child,
　　　and one to clothe it.
And they also took care of feeding the babies
　　　and keeping them clean . . . .

Rabbi Chiyya the Great said:

The angels did not do this,
 but rather, the Holy One, blessed be He,
 in all His glory.

And the babies continued to grow in the field like the plants,
 and they would sneak into their houses
 mixed in with the flocks of sheep . . . .
But how did they know to go to their own parents?
The Holy One, blessed be He, would go with them,
 and show each one his parents' house, saying,
 "Call your father by this name,
 and your mother by this name."

The child would then say to the mother,
 "Don't you remember when you bore me
 in such-and-such a field
 on such-and-such a day
 five months ago?"
And the mother would say,
 "Who raised you?"
And the child would say,
"A certain young man,
 with nice curly hair—
 there is no one like him—
 and he is standing right outside the door.
He brought me here."
And the mother would say to the child,
"Show him to me."
When they went outside,
 looking in all the alleyways,
 everywhere,
 they could not find him.

Thus,
 when they arrived at the Red Sea
 and saw Him,
 the children would point Him out to their mothers, saying,
 "This is my God,
 and I will praise Him"—
 this is the One who raised me—
"This is my God,
 and I will glorify Him." (Exodus 15:2)

This is the meaning of the verse,
"I let you grow like the plants of the field . . . ." (Ezekiel 16:7)

Deuteronomy Rabba,
Devarim 14, Lieberman, p. 14

118. "I will make . . .

> your gates of precious stones [O Jerusalem],
> your surrounding wall of gems." (Isaiah 54:12)

Rabbi Yochanan once sat and explained,
"In the Future,
> the Holy One, blessed be He,
> will bring jewels and pearls thirty cubits by thirty cubits,
> and will cut openings out of them
> that will be ten cubits by twenty cubits,
> and He will set them in the gates of Jerusalem."
One of the students sneered at him, saying,
"Jewels the size of even small doves' eggs are nowhere to be found,
> and you are saying such immense gems will be used?"
A while later, the student was out on a boat.
He saw angels sitting and cutting
> ten by twenty pieces in jewels and pearls
> that were thirty by thirty cubits.
He said,
> "For whom are these?"
They said to him,
"In the Future,
> the Holy One, blessed be He,
> will place them in the gates of Jerusalem."
The student then returned to Rabbi Yochanan and said,
"My teacher—teach!
You teach wonderfully!
I have seen just what you spoke about!"
Rabbi Yochanan said to him,
"Empty one—
> if you hadn't seen it,
> you would not have believed it?
You are one who ridicules the Sages' teachings."
He then stared intensely at the student
> and turned him into a pile of bones.

Bava Batra 75a

101

119. It once happened that Rabbi Elazar the son of Rabbi Shimon
was coming from his teacher's house in Migdal Gedor.
He was riding on a donkey alongside the river,
feeling very proud of himself
because he had studied a great deal of Torah.
He happened to meet a man who was extremely ugly.
The man said,
"Shalom to you, my teacher."
But Rabbi Elazar the son of Rabbi Shimon
did not answer his greeting.
Instead, he said,
" 'How ugly is 'that man'!
Is everyone in your city as ugly as you are?"
The man replied,
"I don't know,
but go and say to the Craftsman who made me,
'How ugly is this utensil you have made!' "
When Rabbi Elazar the son of Rabbi Shimon
realized he had done wrong,
he dismounted from the donkey and said,
"I humble myself before you.
Forgive me."
The man said to him,
"I will not forgive you
until you go to the Craftsman who made me, and say,
'How ugly is this utensil you have made!' "
The rabbi continued walking behind him
until they came to the rabbi's city.
The townspeople came out,
calling out greetings, saying,
"Shalom to you,
my Rabbi, my Rabbi,
my teacher, my teacher."
The man said,
"Whom are you calling,
'My Rabbi, my Rabbi'?"
They said to him,
"We are referring to this one
who is walking behind you."

He said,
>'If this one is a rabbi,
>I hope there will not be many more like him
>among the Jews."

They said to him,
>"Why is that?"

He said to them,
>"He did such-and-such a thing to me."

They said to him,
>"Nevertheless, forgive him,
>because he is a great person for his Torah-knowledge."

He said to them,
>"For your sakes I will forgive him,
>but do not let him get into the habit of doing such things."

Rabbi Elazar the son of Rabbi Shimon
>immediately went into the place of Torah-study and taught,

"A person should always be soft as a reed,
>and not as hard as a cedar.

It is because of this quality
>that reeds have been privileged to be selected
>as pens with which Torahs, Tfillin, and Mezuzot are written."

Ta'anit 20a–b

PHYSICIANS AND HEALING

120. Until the time of Abraham, there were no physical signs of aging . . . .
Until Jacob, no one ever became sick . . . .
Until Elisha, no one ever became sick and then recovered.

Bava Metzia 87a

121. If a person was bitten by a snake or scorpion, it is permitted to whisper a charm on the place where he was bitten—even on Shabbat—in order to give the person peace of mind and to give him psychological strength. Even though the charm provides absolutely no medically therapeutic benefit, nevertheless, since the person is in a dangerous condition, this is permitted so that he will not become distraught.

Maimonides, Mishnah Torah
Laws of Idolatry 11:11

122. The best of physicians inevitably ends up in Hell.

Kiddushin 82a

123. Abba the Therapeutic Blood-letter would receive greetings of peace every day from the Torah-School in the Sky.
Abaye would receive similar greetings, but only once a week, before Shabbat.
Rava, too, would get similar well-wishes, but only once a year—before Yom Kippur.
Abaye was troubled by the particular distinction shown to Abba the Blood-letter.
He was told:
You have not achieved what Abba has achieved.
And what were these things that Abba the Bloodletter did?
When he was performing his operations, he would separate the men from the women.
Furthermore, he had a special gown with slits in it, through which he would put the bleeding instrument. Whenever a woman would come for treatment, he would have her wear this gown, so he would not have to unnecessarily expose her body.
In addition, he had a place—away from the public view—where people could pay their fees. Whoever could pay, would pay there, and whoever could not, would not be embarrassed.

When he would see a sage who could not afford to pay, he would say:
Take this money as a loan and get your strength back.*
One day Abaye sent two sages to investigate the situation.
He gave them seats, gave them food and drink,
    and at night gave them wool mattresses to sleep on.
In the morning they rolled up the mattresses and took them with them.
They went out to the market, where they encountered him.
They said:
How much would you say these are worth, sir?
He said:
They are worth such-and-such.
They said:
Maybe they are worth more?
He said:
That is how much I paid for them.
They said to him:
They are yours . . . . We took them. Forgive us—but what did you suspect?
He said:
I assumed that the Rabbis were involved in the Mitzvah of redeeming some
    captives but were embarrassed to ask me for money.
They said:
Now you should take them back, sir.
He said:
From the moment you took them, I no longer considered them mine. As far
    as I was concerned, they belonged to Tzedakah.

Ta'anit 21b–22a
(With Manuscripts, according to
Dikdukay Sofrim 6:122–124)

Other texts and manuscripts offer the following variations:
If a student of the Sages would come in, he would not take a fee.

And:

When he would see someone who could not afford to pay, he would give that person money,
saying: Go, regain your strength.

ADAM AND EVE

124. When the sun went down
     on the night of the first day
     that Adam had been created,
     he said:
     Woe is me!
     Because I have sinned,
     the world has become dark all around me,
     and the world shall surely return to chaos!
     This is the death
     with which Heaven is punishing me!
     All night he sat and fasted and wept,
     Eve doing the same.
     When dawn began to break,
     he said:
     It was only the nature of things.
     And he got up
     and sacrificed an extraordinary ox
     whose horns were created before its hooves.

Avoda Zara 8a

125. Rabbi Yehuda ben Betraya says:

     Adam used to lounge around the Garden of Eden with angels standing before
     him, roasting meat and chilling wine for him.
     When the serpent came along and saw his magnificent status, he became
     jealous.

Avot DeRabbi Natan A:1

126. At the very moment Eve ate the fruits of the tree,
     she saw the Angel of Death coming towards her.
     She said:
     It appears that I shall be leaving this world,
     and another woman will be created for Adam in my place.
     What shall I do?
     I shall have him also eat.

Avot DeRabbi Natan B:1

127. Rabbi Simon said:

For one hundred thirty years Adam did not have sexual relations with Eve.
Why?
When he saw that he had fathered Cain and Abel,
and that Cain then went and killed Abel—
it wasn't enough that Abel was killed,
but Cain, who killed him, was destined for a life of destruction and desola-
tion, . . .
and thus both, in essence, were destroyed—
what did he do?
He ceased from having sexual relations for one hundred thirty years . . . .
What did the Holy One, blessed be He, then do?
He doubled Adam's lust, and then Adam had relations with Eve,
and Seth was born.
The Holy One, blessed be He, said, "The essential reason I created
My world was that it should be populated."

Deuteronomy Rabba,
Devarim 12
Lieberman, p. 10

FOOD

128. People should not be hot-tempered during a meal.

Shulchan Aruch,
Orach Chaim 170:6

129. One should immediately offer to the waiter anything that is being served that has an aroma and anything else that anyone would have a strong appetite for.

It is a particularly fine practice to give him something immediately from each kind of food.

Shulchan Aruch,
Orach Chaim 169:1

130. One should not share the food with the waiter unless he or she is someone who is certain to recite a blessing.

(Gloss: There are those who are lenient on this issue if he is giving it to a poor person in the form of Tzedakah.)

Shulchan Aruch,
Orach Chaim 169:2,
With Isserles

131. Guests are not allowed to take from their plates and give to the host's child or his servant unless they have obtained permission from the host beforehand.

Shulchan Aruch,
Orach Chaim 170:19

132. People should not drink an entire glassful in one gulp.
And if they do, they are considered gluttons.
Two drinks to a glass is considered proper etiquette.
Three is arrogance.

Gloss: In any event, one may drink from an entire glass in one shot, if the glass is very small.
So, too, a very large glass—
one may drink it in three or four drinks.

Shulchan Aruch,
Orach Chaim 170:8,
With Isserles

133. Rabbi Ammi and Rabbi Assi—
One of them said:

One who has bread in his basket is not the same as
one who does not have bread in his basket.
The other said:

One who can see and eats is not the same as
one who cannot see and eats.

Rav Yosef said:

From this we have a hint that blind people eat,
but do not have complete satisfaction.

Yoma 74b

134. *A person should not say to his friend, "Come and eat with me what you fed me,"—because it would then be like paying back a debt.*

It would appear to be like a loan, and there is a chance he would feed him more, and that would be like paying interest. But it is permitted to say to him, "Come and eat with me, and I will eat with you some other time,"—then it is all right to eat even a bigger meal with the other person.

Gloss by Isserles to
Shulchan Aruch,
Orach Chaim 170:13

SHABBAT

135. Friday night dreams have no effective substance to them.

Yoma 83b

136. One should enjoy a number of fruits, delicacies, and fragrances on Shabbat, in order to complete the required hundred blessings a day.

Gloss: If one normally takes an afternoon nap, one should not do away with it on Shabbat, since this constitutes a pleasure for him.

Shulchan Aruch,
Orach Chaim, 290:1
With Isserles

137. Some authorities state that, if eating will harm someone, and consequently it is a pleasure for him not to eat—then he should not eat on Shabbat.

Shulchan Aruch,
Orach Chaim 288:2

138. Rabbi Yitzchak said:

Sunshine on the Shabbat is an act of Tzedakah for the benefit of the poor.

Ta'anit 8b

139. It was taught:
It was said of Shammai the Elder
that all his life he would eat in honor of Shabbat . . . .
If he found a fine animal, he would say,
"This is for Shabbat."
If he found another one nicer than the first,
he would set it aside for Shabbat
and eat the first one at some other time.
Hillel, however, had a different approach—
all his actions were for the sake of Heaven,
as the verse says,
"Blessed be God every day." (Psalm 68:20)

Betzah 16a

140. Ezra instituted ten regulations
[Among them are the following]:
That the Torah should be read in public on Shabbat afternoon;
That the Torah should be read in public on Mondays and Thursdays;
That the courts should sit in session on Mondays and Thursdays;
That clothes should be washed on Thursdays;
That garlic should be eaten Friday evening.

Bava Kamma 82a

141. It is a Mitzvah to make breakthroughs in Torah-study on Shabbat. Someone who is not sufficiently skilled to do so, at least should study some material he had not studied previously.

Mishna Berura to
Shulchan Aruch,
Orach Chaim 290:1,
In the name of the Zohar

142. It is permitted to fast on Shabbat for a bad dream—so that the heavenly decree will be torn up.
The person then has to fast on Sunday, in order to be forgiven for having ignored the Mitzvah of Taking Delight in the Shabbat.
If he is weak, however, and cannot fast two days in a row, he should not fast on Sunday, but rather on some other day.
. . . .
Some authorities rule that a dream-fast on Shabbat is not permitted unless he saw the dream three times.
And some authorities rule that, in our day, people should not fast these dream-fasts, because we are no longer experts in the interpretation of dreams, and are unable, therefore, to know which is a good dream and which one is harmful.

Shulchan Aruch,
Orach Chaim 288:4–5

143. It is customary to cover the knives at the table when it is time to recite the blessings after the meal.

The custom is not to do this on Shabbat and holidays.

Shulchan Aruch,
Orach Chaim 180:5

111

PRAYER

144. Abaye said:

You should always associate yourself with the community [by reciting prayers in the plural grammatical form].

Berachot 29b–30a

145. Rav Chiya bar Ashi said in the name of Rav:

One whose mind is not at ease should not pray . . . .
Rabbi Chanina would not pray on a day when he was distressed . . . .
Shmuel did not pray in a house where there were alcoholic beverages.

Eruvin 65a

146. Rabbi Iddi the son of Rabbi Shimon said in the name of Rabbi Yossa:

People should not pray while standing on a high place.

*Jerusalem Talmud
Berachot 2:3*

147. Rabbi Iddi the son of Rabbi Shimon said in the name of Rabbi Yochanan:

People should not pray if they have to go to the bathroom.

*Jerusalem Talmud
Berachot 2:3*

148. Rabbi Yehoshua ben Levi said:

When a person is about to begin praying, he should sit down twice—
    once before he begins
    and once again afterwards.
Beforehand, he should recite,
"Happy are they who sit in Your house;
    they are forever praising You." (Psalm 84:5)
Afterwards, he should recite,
"The righteous shall certainly praise Your name;
    the upright shall sit in Your presence." (Psalm 140:14)

*Jerusalem Talmud,
Berachot 5:1*

A MISCELLANY

149. When the Holy One, blessed be He, told Moses to slaughter the Passover lamb, Moses said to him, "Master of the world, how can I do this thing? Don't you know that lambs are gods to the Egyptians?" . . . .

The Holy One, blessed be He, said, "I swear by your life, the Jews shall not leave Egypt until they slaughter the Egyptians' gods right before their very eyes, so that I can demonstrate to them that their gods are worthless."

Exodus Rabba 16:3

150. Our Rabbis have taught:

What does a person say while dancing before a bride?
The School of Shammai says,
 "The words must correspond to the bride."
The School of Hillel says,
 "[For all brides we say the same formula]—'A beautiful and charming
  bride!' "
The School of Shammai said to the School of Hillel,
 "But suppose she were lame or blind—
 do we still say to her,
 'A beautiful and charming bride'?—
But the Torah has said,
 "Keep your distance from lying words."
The School of Hillel said to the School of Shammai,
 "According to what you say,
 what do we say to someone who just made a bad purchase?
 Do we praise it, or do we disparage it?
 Surely you would say that we praise it."
From this the sages stated,
 "People should always be pleasant in their relations with others."

Ketubot 17a

151. Rabbi Yitzchak said:

Blessings are not found except in things hidden from the eye.

. . . .

It was taught in the school of Rabbi Yishmael:
Blessings are not found except in things over which the eye has no control.

. . . .

Our Rabbis have taught:

. . . .

Blessings are not to be found in things that can be weighed, nor measured,
  nor counted, but rather only in things hidden from the eye.

Ta'anit 8b

152. Rabbi Chanania, the Assistant to the Priests, says:

For the forty years previous to the destruction of the Temple
    and the burning of the Holy Precincts,
    the people of Jerusalem would lock the Temple gates
    and awaken the next morning to find them open . . . .
Once the Children of the High Priests saw
    that the Temple was indeed destroyed
    and the Holy Precincts burned,
    they took the keys,
    went up to the top of the Holy Precincts,
    and threw the keys towards Heaven, saying,
"Here are the keys back —
    the ones you gave us.
We were not faithful guardians,
    and, therefore, not entitled to enjoy the special treasures
    of The King."
They then held tightly to each other
    and ran into the fire
    and were burned to death.

Avot DeRabbi Natan B:7, End

153. Rabbi Shimon bar Yochai's students asked him:

Why didn't the Manna come down for the Jews only once a year [rather than
on every week-day]?
He said to them:

I will explain it by a parable—
This is like a human king who has only one son,
    and who provided the son's food only by annual allotments.
As a result, the son would visit his father only once a year.
So the king changed his method,
    giving his son food every day instead.
As a result, the son visited his father every day.
So, too, with the Jews—
A person who had four or five children would worry, saying,
    "Maybe there will be no Manna tomorrow,
    and all of them will die of hunger."
Consequently, all of them turned their hearts regularly towards their
    Father in Heaven.

Yoma 76a

154. Rav Yehuda said in the name of Rav:

The forty-two letter [mystical] Name of God is not to be transmitted to anyone unless he is unassuming, humble, middle-aged, without a bad temper,
not given to alcoholic indulgence, and forebearing.

Anyone who knows the Name, and is careful about it, and watches it with
purity is beloved in Heaven Above, and pleasing on the earth below, is held
in awe by God's creatures, and inherits two worlds—this world and the
Future world.

Kiddushin 71a

155. It is customary to say to someone who is wearing a new piece of clothing,
"Tevaleh U'Techadesh—May you live to wear it out and buy a new one."

Gloss by Isserles to
Shulchan Aruch,
Orach Chaim 223:6

156. Rabbi Dosta'i the son of Rabbi Yossi says:

Why did God not create hot springs in Jerusalem like the hot springs of
   Tiberias?
So that nobody should say to another, "Let us go up to Jerusalem. Even if we
   go only for one quick dip in the hot springs, that will be enough."
The end result would be that people would not be going up to Jerusalem for
   its own sake.

Sifre on Numbers,
Beha'alotecha, 89

157. Rav Yehuda said in the name of Shmuel in the name of Rabbi Meir:

While I was studying Torah with Rabbi Akiva, . . .
I once went to Rabbi Yishmael.
He said to me,
"My son, what work do you do?"
I said to him,
"I am a scribe."
He said to me,
"My son, be very careful, because your work is the Work of Heaven.
If you add or subtract a single letter, you may find that you have destroyed
   the entire world."

Sotah 20a

158. Rabbi Chanina ben Dosa says:

Nothing went to waste from the ram [that Abraham sacrificed in place of
   Isaac]—
its ashes became the base for the inner altar of the Temple,
its ten sinews became the strings for the lute that David used to play,
its hide became Elijah's belt,
and its two horns—
God used the left one as a Shofar at Mt. Sinai,
and the right one—larger than the left—will be blown in the future
to gather in all the Jews in exile to Israel.

Pirke DeRebbi Eliezer 31

159. Rav Yehuda said in the name of Rav:

In any city where there are many hills,
the people and the animals who live there live only half a normal lifespan.
Do you really mean:
Live half a normal lifespan?
Rather say:
They age twice as quickly.

Eruvin 56a

160. Caesar once said to Rabbi Tanchuma:

Come, let us all become one people.

He replied:

Fine. But since we are circumcised, we cannot be like you. You, therefore,
become circumcised and be like us.

Caesar answered:

You have given an excellent answer. However, anyone who wins an argument with the Emperor must be thrown into the arena with wild beasts.
They threw him in, but the beasts did not eat him.

A certain heretic observed:

They did not eat him because they were not hungry.
They threw the heretic in, and the beasts ate him.

Sanhedrin 39a

161. Rabbi Yirmiah bar Elazar said:

[The builders of the Tower of Babel] were divided into three groups—
One said, "We'll go up and live there."
Another said, "We'll go up there and worship idols."
The third said, "We'll go up there and make war."

Sanhedrin 109a

162. Rabbi Shmuel bar Nachmani said in the name of Rabbi Yonatan:

A person who purchases a city in the Land of Israel may be forced to purchase roads leading into it from all four directions—because of the benefit it will bring for the development of the Land of Israel.

Bava Kamma 80b

163. When a Psalm begins with "To David, a Psalm"—
it means that
first God's Intimate Presence rested on him,
and then he composed the song.
When a Psalm begins with "A Psalm, to David"—
it means that
first he composed the Psalm
and then God's Intimate Presence rested on him.

Pesachim 117a

164. A person should not raise a dog unless it is on a leash.

Bava Kamma 79b

165. Rabbi Natan says:

What is the source of the rule that states that a person should not keep a mean dog or broken-down ladder in his house?
The verse in the Torah states, "You should not bring bloodguilt on your house." (Deuteronomy 22:8)

Ketubot 41b

THE FLYING LETTERS

166. Moses took the tablets and began down the mountain.
The writing on the tablets carried themselves and Moses, too.
When the writing saw the tambourines and the dancing and the Golden Calf,
they ran off and flew away from the tablets.
The tablets became too heavy for Moses—
he could no longer hold himself up,
nor could he handle the tablets.
So he threw them down,
and they shattered.

Pirke DeRebbi Eliezer, 45

167. Why did Moses break the tablets?
Because the writing had alrady flown off of them . . . .
That's why he broke them.
What is this situation like?
It is like a postman who was going into a certain province
carrying the king's proclamation.
While he was crossing a river,
the letters fell in the water,
and the words were erased.
What did the postman do?
He tore them up.
As the verse indicates,
"And I saw how you had sinned against the Lord your God." (Deuteronomy
    9:16)
What did he see?
He saw that the letters had flown away,
so he broke the tablets.

Tanchuma, Ekev 11
Eshkol Edition

168. Rabbi Meir said:

Once Moses saw what the Israelites did with the Golden Calf,
he immediately looked at the tablets
and saw that the writing had flown away.
So he threw the tablets to the ground.
What is this situation like?
It is like a man who had a candle in his hand,
but it went out.
Once he saw that the candle had gone out,
he said,
"Why am I holding this?"
and he threw it away.
So, too,
once the Israelites did what they did with the Golden Calf,
the writing flew away from the tablets.
Moses asked,
"Why do I need these tablets?"
Then the Torah says,
"And Moses became angry.
He threw the tablets from his hands
and shattered them at the base of the mountain." (Exodus 32:19)

Midrash HaGadol,
Exodus 32:19

COMMUNITY LEADERSHIP

169. When the members of his community wanted to appoint Rabbi Akiva their leader, he said:

> Let me discuss it with my household.
> They followed him and overheard them saying:
>
> If you take the position,
> know that they will curse you and despise you.

Jerusalem Talmud,
Peah 8:6

170. Even though Rabbi Elazar ben Azariah assumed a position of distinguished leadership in the community—nevertheless, he lived a long life.

Jerusalem Talmud,
Berachot 1:6

171. The Holy One, blessed be He, weeps every day over these three kinds of people:
For one who is able to be involved in Torah study but is not involved;
for one who is unable to be involved but is involved, nevertheless,
and for a community leader who is arrogant towards his constituents.

Chagiga 5b

172. Rabbi Yochanan said:

> Woe to those in positions of communal leadership,
> for the job buries those who take on the position . . . .
> We see that every prophet outlived four kings.

Pesachim 87b

173. Rabbi Yehoshua ben Levi said:

> I once learned eighty laws concerning graves that had been ploughed over, but, because I was so involved in community affairs, I forget them all.

Ecclesiastes Rabba 7:7, 1

174. *(In the Book of Numbers 11:24–30, the story is told that God took some of the spirit that rested upon Moses and put it on the seventy elders. As a result, the elders began to prophesy. Two people, Eldad and Medad, who had remained in the Israelite camp, were also filled with this spirit, and prophesied within the camp. Joshua, concerned about this turn of events, goes to Moses and urges him to restrain the two of them. The Talmud offers an interesting twist to Joshua's request.)*

Joshua said to Moses,
"Heap on them community responsibilities, and they will stop by themselves."

(Tosafot, one of the Talmudic commentaries, interprets as follows:)
Their ability to prophesy will disappear,
because God's Intimate Presence is not felt in sadness—
but rather only in joy.

Sanhedrin 17a

DEATH AND DYING

175. Rav Chanan bar Rava said in the name of Rav:

The very day that Abraham died,
all the distinguished leaders of the world's nations stood in line to express
    words of comfort, saying,
"Woe to the world that has lost its leader!
and woe to the ship that has lost its pilot!"

Bava Batra 91a–b

176. When Hillel the Elder died, they lamented:

Woe for the loss of such a pious person [Chassid]!
Woe for the loss of such a humble person [Anav]!

Sanhedrin 11a

177. This is the way things are in life:

When the righteous are born, nobody is aware of it,
but when they die, everyone feels it.

Ecclesiastes Rabba 7:1, 4

178. One of the Torah-Masters taught:

The day Rabbi Akiva died, Rabbi Yehuda the Prince was born.
When Rabbi Yehuda the Prince died, Rav Yehuda was born.
When Rav Yehuda died, Rava was born.
When Rava died, Rav Ashi was born,
which indicates that no Righteous Person dies until a similar one is created,
as the Biblical verse shows,
"The sun rises, and the sun sets." (Ecclesiastes 1:5)

Kiddushin 72b

179. When Rabban Yochanan ben Zakkai's son died, his students came to comfort him.

. . . .

Rabbi Elazar ben Arach sat down in front of him and said:

123

I am going to tell you a parable.
To what may we compare your situation?
It is like a man to whom the king has entrusted something to be taken care of.
Every single day the man would weep intensely, saying:

Woe is me! When shall I be free of this thing, and once again be at peace?

So, too, with you, my teacher—
you had a son who studied the written Torah completely and the Mishna,
and all the legal and non-legal materials, and he left the world without sin.
Now that you have returned that which was entrusted to you, it is appropriate
for you to be comforted.

Rabba Yochanan said to him:

Elazar, my son, you have comforted me the way people ought to give comfort.

Avot DeRabbi Natan A:14

180. Rabbi Yossi said:

May I be privileged to be among those who die in the midst of performing a Mitzvah.

Shabbat 118b

181. The dead are not to be buried in expensive shrouds—
even if the person was a distingushed leader of the Jews (*Nasi*)

Shulchan Aruch,
Yoreh De'ah 352:1

182. We do not bury a wicked person (*Rasha*) next to a righteous one (*Tzaddik*),
nor even a considerably wicked one (*Rasha Chamur*) next to one who lived
only a somewhat sinful life (*Rasha Kal*).
Similarly, we do not bury a righteous person (*Tzaddik*)—
and even more so, an average person (*Baynoni*)—
next to an extraordinarily saintly person (*Chassid Muflag*).
However, we do bury those who have returned to the Jewish way (*Ba'al
Teshuvah*)
next to a completely righteous person (*Tzaddik Gamur*).

Shulchan Aruch,
Yoreh De'ah 362:5,
According to text of The Shach

183. Rabbi Yossi the son of Rabbi Bun said:

Those who stand in the presence of the dead [at a funeral]
are not standing in honor of the deceased,
but rather in honor of those who are performing an act of lovingkindness
for the deceased.

Jerusalem Talmud,
Bikkurim 3:3

184. What is the minimum age of a child for whom a eulogy should be recited?
For a poor family—from age five.
For a wealthy family—from age six.
The children of elderly parents are in the same category as children of the poor.

Shulchan Aruch,
Yoreh De'ah 344:4

185. "A time to weep"—at the time of mourning;
"And a time to laugh"—after the mourning.
"A time to wail"—at the time of mourning;
"And a time to dance"—after the mourning.

Ecclesiastes Rabba 3:3, 1
(Based on Ecclesiastes 3:4)

186. Rabbi Alexandri said in the name of Rabbi Chiyya bar Abba,
and some say Rabbi Yehoshua ben Levi said:

When a person's time comes to die, anyone or anything can control the
      situation.
Rav derived this from the verse,
"This day they stand to carry out Your rulings,
for all are Your servants." (Psalm 119:91)
Shmuel once saw a frog carry a scorpion across a river.
The scorpion bit a particular man and killed him.

Nedarim 41a

187. Rabbi Elazar was sitting in the bathroom when a Roman came along and made him stand up.
The Roman sat down in his place,
and a snake came and bit him,
killing him.

Ecclesiastes Rabba 5:8, 5

188. The dead say to one another,
"Tomorrow they will be with us, and yet they cause us trouble?

Jerusalem Talmud
Berachot 2:3

189. It is permitted to ask a deathly ill person to swear to appear to him after death, in order to tell him whatever he asks.

(GLOSS: There are those who permit doing this even after the person has died, as long as he does not make the body swear, but rather only the spirit.)

Shulchan Aruch,
Yoreh De'ah 179:14,
With Isserles

BOOK THREE

TABLE OF CONTENTS: Book Three

INTRODUCTION

The publication of this volume brings to a total of more than five hundred the number of selections I have translated from traditional Jewish texts. I have continued to choose items that relate to the theme of Torah and Menschlichkeit in a format suitable for individual, small-group, and classroom study. Jewish values remain the central topic throughout, as is seen from Selection #1, which, I believe, sets the tone: our real occupation in life is Mitzvot and Menschlichkeit, and what our so-called "occupations" are are of relatively minor importance. It is hoped that this third anthology will further encourage people to pursue Jewish study more deeply and extensively, always keeping in mind that the texts are intended to lead towards a certain pattern of living. Whether or not this quality of Menschlichkeit is ultimately achievable is secondary to the fact that this ought to be the goal and purpose of Torah study, worth striving for, worth failing over, worth striving for again.

This volume contains an extended section on the life of Rabbi Akiva, a hero and role model of mine for years. It is hoped that once the student has begun studying his life (and these texts are barely a beginning), he or she will continue to examine the lives of the other Talmudic Rebbis, seeking out qualities and character traits that should be integrated into The Twentieth Century Soul.

The past two years (since the first volume was published) have proven that many have overcome their fear of the volume and immensity of Torah texts (see Selection #102), and their apparent difficulty. At study sessions I will often ask the students to take a few minutes to leaf through and pick out a text or two that might interest them. *Even students who have had no Talmudic training, and have spent only an hour or two studying these texts in a group setting, have found it relatively easy to pause, think about, and enjoy the material.* It is my hope that this scenario will be repeated in many places for many more people.

With the publication of this volume, I have decided to add three elements: (1) A topical index to all three volumes has been appended, prepared by my teacher, student, and friend, Beth Huppin, in order to allow the student to pursue further interplay among the many selections. (2) At the request of many friends, a separate pamphlet is being offered, in rather crude form, of the xeroxes of my note cards in Hebrew and Aramaic, of many of these texts (all of the selections from Book Three and about one-third to one-half of Books One and Two). . . . transcriptions of the original texts. (3) Furthermore, and I believe most important, The Town House Press is issuing a larger-print edition of all three books, for those individuals who have visual difficulties and need access to larger print. Carolyn Bondy of Silver Spring, Maryland, approached me after one of my talks, and explained to me that

131

she enjoyed the material very much, but could not read it because the print was too small. As a result, we are offering this service, and encourage others who are publishing Jewish books to do the same. I am grateful to Mrs. Bondy for bringing this to my attention.

To all of us—Many Years Of Torah Study—with Passion and Simcha, and Joy Deep in the Soul.

Danny Siegel
January 8, 1985

WHERE HEAVEN AND EARTH TOUCH

1. "Open the Gates of Righteousness for me." (Psalm 118:19)
   [At the Time of Judgment] in the Future World
   everyone will be asked,
   "What was your occupation?"
   If the person answers,
   "I used to feed the hungry,"
   they will say to him,
   "This is God's gate;
   you, who fed the hungry, may enter."
   . . .
   "I used to give water to those who were thirsty,"—
   they will say to him,
   "This is God's gate;
   you, who gave water to those who were thirsty, may enter."
   . . .
   "I used to clothe the naked,"
   they will say to him,
   "This is God's gate,
   you, who clothed the naked, may enter."
   . . . .
   and similarly with those who raised orphans,
   and who performed the Mitzvah of Tzedakah,
   and who performed acts of caring, lovingkindness.

   Midrash Psalms 118:17
   Buber, p. 486

TORAH I

2. Shimon, the son of Rabban Gamliel, says:

. . . .

The essential thing is not study,
but Mitzvah-deeds.

Sayings of the Fathers 1:17

3. Rav said:

The Mitzvot were given
in order to refine human beings.

Leviticus Rabbi 13:3
Margoliot 2:277

4. Rabbi Yossi says:

It is not the place that honors the person,
but the person that honors the place.

Ta'anit 21b

5. Rava had a favorite saying:
The ultimate purpose of Torah-wisdom
is a turning-toward-Menschlichkeit [Teshuvah]
and good deeds.
It makes no sense
that a person should study the Written and Oral Torah
and then kick his father or mother or Rebbi
or someone who is greater than he is in wisdom and stature.*

. . . .

And whoever studies Torah for reasons other than these—
it were better that he not have even been created.

Berachot 17a

*Others interpret: "Or someone who is greater than he is in wisdom or in number of students."

6. Rabbi Chiyya taught:

People should study Torah with the intention of doing the Mitzvot,
and not without that intention,
because someone who studies,
but does not intend to perform Mitzvot—
it were better that he not even be created.

Rabbi Yochanan said:

People who study without any intention of performing Mitzvot—
it were better that their placentas had turned over on their faces [at birth],
and they not entered the world at all.

Leviticus Rabba,
BeChukotai 35:7
Margoliot 4:826

7. The verse,
"A cord made of three strands is not readily broken" (Ecclesiastes 4:12)
refers to someone involved in three things:
The Written Torah,
The Oral Torah,
and Menschlich living [Derech Eretz].

Tosefta Kiddushin 1, end

8. Rav Huna said:

Anyone who is involved only in Torah-study
[but does not also perform Deeds of Lovingkindness]—
that person is like someone who has no God.

Avoda Zara 17b

9. Rav Pappa said:

The verse states, "Study them and observe them!" (Deuteronomy 5:1)—
Whoever is involved in performing the Mitzvot,
is also considered to be involved in Torah-study.
Whoever is not involved in performing the Mitzvot, however,
is not considered to be involved in Torah-study.

Yevamot 109b

10. Rabbi Simon and Rabbi Elazar were sitting
    when Rabbi Ya'akov bar Acha walked by.

    One of them said to the other:
    Let us rise in his presence,
    for here is a person who fears wrongdoing!

    The other replied:
    Let us rise in his presence,
    for here is a person who knows Torah!

    The first one answered back:
    I have told you "Here is a man who fears wrongdoing"
    and you tell me only "He knows Torah"?*

Shabbat 31b

*A relatively secondary quality.

11. Rabbi Elazar HaModa'i says: . . .

    [If you will heed the Lord your God diligently,]
    doing what is upright in His sight, (Exodus 15:26)—
    this refers to business affairs.
    It teaches us that
    whoever is honest in his business,
    and other people find it delightful to deal with him,*
    it is considered as though he had personified the entire Torah.

Mechilta, Beshallach,
Massechta DeVayassa 1,
Lauterbach II:95-96

*Or: and [as a result,] other people find it delightful to deal with him.

12. Rabbi Chanina bar Pappa explained:

The angel in charge of pregnancy is called Lylah.
He takes the drop of sperm
and stands it before the Holy One, blessed be He, and asks,
"Master of the Universe!
This drop—what will become of it?
Will it be strong or weak?
Wise or foolish?
Rich or poor?"
But he does not ask
if it will be wicked or righteous,—
which follows Rabbi Chanina's opinion,
as Rabbi Chanina said:

Everything is in the hands of Heaven
except for the fear of Heaven.

Niddah 16b

13. "A time to embrace" (Ecclesiastes 3:5)—
If you see a group of the righteous standing there,
stand and hug them and kiss them and hug them again.
"A time to refrain from embracing" (Ecclesiastes 3:5)—
If you see a group of evil people,
stay away from them and from anyone who resembles them.

Ecclesiastes Rabba 3:5,1

14. Abbaye said:

Woe not only to the wicked,
but woe, too, to his neighbor!
Good things for the righteous,
and good things, too, for his neighbor!

Sukkah 56b

15. It was taught in another source [Mishna Shabbat 16:1]:
[If there is a fire on Shabbat,]
we save the container holding a Sefer Torah
along with the Sefer Torah,
and the container holding Tfillin
along with the Tfillin.
This teaches you:
Happy are the righteous,
and happy are those who are attached to them.
this is the meaning of the verse,
"God remembered Noah
and all the beasts and all the cattle
that were with him in the ark." (Genesis 8:1)
All of them were saved because of Noah.

Tanchuma, Vayyera 9

16. "One who associates with sages becomes wise" (Proverbs 13:20)—

What is this person like?
He is like someone who goes into a perfume-maker's shop.
Even though he did not take anything or give anything,
nevertheless he takes out with him a wonderful aroma.
So, too, anyone who associates with the righteous—
he takes with him some of their good ways and acts.

"But one who associates with fools comes to grief" (Proverbs 13:20)—

What is this person like?
He is like someone who goes into a tannery.
Even though he did not give anything or take anything,
nevertheless he takes out with him a horrible stench.
So, too, anyone who associates with bad people—
he takes with him some of their evil ways and acts.

Pirke DeRebbi Eliezer 25

17. Rav Nachman bar Yitzchak said:

. . . .

[In the Future World]
not everyone will be entitled to the light,
nor will everyone be entitled to the joy.
The light will be for the righteous,
and joy will be for the upright.
The light will be for the righteous, as it is written,
"Light is sown for the righteous," (Psalm 97:11)
and joy for the upright, as it is written,
"and joy for the upright." (Psalm 97:11)

Ta'anit 15a

18. A Halachah:

When a Jew goes up to read from the Torah,
he is not allowed to do so until he recites a blessing.
First comes the blessing, then he reads.

So, too, with Moses, when he was privileged to be the first
to receive the Torah—
before he read it, he recited a blessing.

Rabbi Elazar asked:

What was the blessing Moses recited before reading the Torah?
Blessed are You, O Lord, our God, Ruler of the Universe,
Who has chosen this Torah, has made it holy,
and has taken delight in those who fulfill it.

He did not say:

"those who work hard at studying it",
nor "those who think deeply about it and expound upon it",
but rather—"those who fulfill it",
those who live out their lives according to the words of Torah.

Deuteronomy Rabba,
Bracha 11:6

19. Rav Huna said:

If a person failed and transgressed,
and deserved a death penalty at the hands of God,
what should he do to survive?
If it was his practice to recite one page of the Written Torah,
let him recite two;
to recite a chapter of the Oral Torah,
let him recite two;
and if he wasn't able to manage
either the Written or the Oral Torah,
what should he do to survive?
Let him become a communal leader
or a Tzedakah collector,
and, as a result, he will live.
If the verse had stated,
"Cursed be the person who does not study
[the terms of this Teaching]"—
there would have been no chance for survival.
But the verse says instead,
"Cursed be the person who does not *uphold*
[the terms of this Teaching."] (Deuteronomy 27:26)—

Leviticus Rabba 25:1
Margoliot 3:568-569

HUMAN DIGNITY, HUMILITY, ARROGANCE, . . .

20. Rabbi Eliezer says:

Let other people's dignity be as precious to you as your own.

Sayings of the Fathers 2:15

21. No one should say,
"Just as I have been humiliated,
so, too, let others be humiliated."

Rabbi Tanchuma said:

If you do so,
know Whom you are humiliating,
[for the verse says]—
"He made him in the likeness of God." (Genesis 5:1)

Genesis Rabba 24, end
Buber 1:237

22. One who curses oneself or another person,
using God's name or substitute names,
transgresses a negative commandment.
. . . .
Rabbi Yannai said:

And everyone agrees about cursing oneself,
because it is written,
"Be careful about yourself,
and watch yourself with great care." (Deuteronomy 4:9)
. . . .
And about cursing others,
because it is written,
"Do not curse the deaf." (Leviticus 19:14)

Shevu'ot 35a, 36a

23. "Do not ascend My altar by steps,
whereby your nakedness may be exposed." (Exodus 20:26)
Here is a "minor to major" logical inference:
The stones of the altar have no sense
of what is proper or not proper,
and yet the Holy One, blessed be He, said,
"Do not treat them disrespectfully."
Is it not right, therefore,
that with other human beings—
who are created in the image
of the One Who spoke and the World came to be—
is it not right
that they should be treated with dignity?

Mechilta, Yitro 11, end

24. Resh Lakish said:

"The spirit of God hovered over the waters" (Genesis 1:2)
refers to the spirit of the first human being.

Midrash Psalms 139:5

25. Rabbi Elazar ben Shamu'a's students asked him:
To what do you attribute your longevity?

He replied:
[Among other things,] I never walked in a fashion that implied
that I was walking on the heads of the holy people.

Rabbi Nechunia ben HaKana's students asked him:
To what do you attribute your longevity?

He replied:
[Among other things,] I never did anything that would bring me honor
by humiliating someone else.

Rabbi Zera's students asked him:
To what do you attribute your longevity?

He replied:
[Among other things,] I never lost my temper in my house, . . .
and I never found pleasure in someone else's misfortunes or failures.

Megillah 27b-28a

26. Rav Chisda said,
and some report that Mar Ukbah said:

The Holy One, blessed be He, says
about an arrogant person,
"He and I can't live in the same world,"
as the verse states,
". . . I cannot stand haughty and proud people."* (Psalm 101:5)

Sotah 5a

*The Talmud has a play on words in the Hebrew, yielding an interpretation from the verse—
"I can't live with him."

27. Our Rabbis have taught:

There are four kinds of people who are called "wicked"—
One who raises his hand to hit another person,
even though he did not hit him,
he is still called "wicked" . . .
One who borrows money but does not repay . . .
One who is arrogant
and does not act with humility
in the presence of someone who is greater . . .
And one who is out always looking to start an argument.

Tanchuma Korach 21,
Buber II:91-92

28. There are certain personality traits
that a person is prohibited to deal with
by the Rule of Moderation.
Rather, he should stay as far away from them
as is humanly possible.

One specific trait—arrogance.
The Good Way is not that a person should be only humble,
but rather . . . *extremely* humble.
That is why Moses is referred to as "very humble" (Numbers 12:3),
and not just "humble."
The sages, therefore, have commanded,
"Be very, very humble." (Sayings of the Fathers 4:4)
Furthermore, they have said that
anyone who is arrogant denies God's existence (Sotah 4b),
as the verse states,
"If you become arrogant,
you will forget the Lord, your God." (Deuteronomy 8:14)
Furthermore, they have said,
"Anyone who is arrogant should be excommunicated" (Sotah 5a)—
even a little bit of arrogance.

Another instance—anger.
It is an extremely terrible personality trait,
and a person would do well to stay as far away from it
as is humanly possible.
. . . .
Our early sages have said,
"Anyone who becomes angry—
it is as though he worships idols."*
And they have said that
anyone who becomes angry—
if he is a sage—
his wisdom will leave him.
And if he is a prophet—
his prophecy will leave him. (Pesachim 66b)
And irascible people's lives
cannot really be called "living."

Maimonides, Mishnah Torah,
Hilchot De'ot 2:3

*The exact wording of. this source is difficult to ascertain. See the commentaries.

TZEDAKAH

29. Every year, Rabbi Elazar ben Azaryah would give twelve thousand calves from his flocks as tithes.

Shabbat 54b

30. Rabbi Abba said in the name of Rabbi Shimon ben Lakish:

One who lends money [to the poor]
is greater than one who just gives it.
And one who forms a partnership
is the greatest of all.

Shabbat 63a

31. When it comes to giving Tzedakah,
there are four kinds of personalities:
One who wants to give,
but doesn't want others to—
he resents the Mitzvah-work of others.
One who wants others to give,
but not himself—
he is greedy.
One who wants to give,
and that others should also give—
he is saintly.
One who doesn't want to give,
and doesn't want others to give either—
he is downright wicked.

Sayings of the Fathers 5:16

32. "Do not rob the poor because he is poor." (Proverbs 22:22)

Our Rabbis have taught:

What is this verse really speaking about?
If the person is poor,
what could he possibly be robbing him of?
Rather, the verse must be speaking of
the Gifts to the Poor that the Torah requires the person to give—
the Gleanings, Forgotten Sheaves of grain, and Corners of the Field,
and the Poor Person's Tithe.
The Holy One, blessed be He, issued a warning
that a person should not rob him
of these gifts which are rightfully his
because he is poor.
His poverty is as much as he can handle.
Is it not enough that the wealthy person is comfortable.
and the poor person is in pain—
and yet he would steal from him
what the Holy One, blessed be He, gave to him?!

Numbers Rabba 5:2

33a. Rabbi Yonah said:

The verse doesn't say,
"Happy is the one who *gives* to the poor,"
but rather,
"Happy is the one who *uses his insight when giving* [משכיל]
    to the poor," (Psalm 41:2)
meaning—
one who uses all his faculties when considering how to do the
    Mitzvah of Tzedakah.

Jerusalem Talmud,
Pe'ah 8:8

33b. Rabbi Yonah said:

The verse doesn't say,

"Happy is the one who *gives* to the poor,"

but rather,

"Happy is the one who *uses his insight when giving* [מַשְׂכִּיל]
    to the poor," (Psalm 41:2)

meaning —

consider this person carefully to discover which way is best to
    be privileged to do this Tzedakah-Mitzvah in this particular
    situation.

Leviticus Rabba 34:1
Margoliot 4:773

34. When Mar Ukba was dying, he said:

Bring me my Tzedakah-records.

When he discovered that the accounts showed he had given away seven
thousand gold Sianian dinars, he said:

These are meager provisions for such a long journey.

He then gave away half his money to Tzedakah.

But how could he do this?

Did not Rabbi Ila'i say in Usha:

A person should not spend more than a fifth on Tzedakah?

That rule only applies during a person's lifetime,

in order to prevent the person from becoming poor himself,

but since death makes this issue irrelevant,

we have no objection [to people giving more at that time].

Ketubot 67b

35a. If a person says,

"I am giving this coin to Tzedakah

so that my child will live"

or "so that I will make it into the Future World" —

that person is a complete Tzaddik [Righteous Person].

Pesachim 8a-b
1st Translation

35b. If a person says,
"I am giving this coin to Tzedakah
so that my child will live"
or "so that I will make it into the Future World"—
that is an act of complete Tzedakah.

Pesachim 8a-b
(According to text of Aruch)
2nd Translation

36. "And they that lead the many to righteousness
will be like the stars for ever and ever" (Daniel 12:3)—
this refers to Tzedakah collectors; . . .
this refers to people who teach Torah to little children.

Bava Batra 8b

37. Rabbi Yochanan said:

Every day, the Holy One, blessed be He,
sings the praises of three kinds of people—
single people who live in a city and do not sin,
poor people who return lost articles to their rightful owners,
and wealthy people who do Tzedakah quietly.*

Pesachim 113a

*Literally, "who tithe their produce quietly."

38. Rabbi Yudan said in the name of Rabbi Elazar:

Three things—
prayer, Tzedakah, and turning-to-Menschlichkeit [Teshuvah]—
eliminate [unfavorable heavenly] decrees.
And all three of these can be derived from a single verse:
"When My people, who bear My name,
humble themselves, pray,
seek out My face,
and turn from their evil ways,
I will hear in My heavens,
and will forgive their sins,
and heal their land" (II Chronicles 7:14)—
"pray"—this refers to prayer;
"seek out My face"—this refers to Tzedakah,
as it is written elsewhere,
"I, through Tzedakah, shall see Your face" (Psalm 17:15);
and "turn from their evil ways"—this is turning-to-Menschlichkeit.
And what is the conclusion of the verse?
"I will hear from My heavens,
and forgive their sins."

Pesikta D'Rav Kahana
BaYom HaShmini Atzeret 28:3

MONEY

39. A reputation is preferable to great wealth,
Grace is better than silver and gold. (Proverbs 22:1)

See how important a good name is in the world!
Even if a person has a thousand gold dinars,
but didn't acquire a good reputation,
he did not really acquire anything at all.

Midrash Proverbs 22:1

40. When Rabbi Simon bar Zevid died,
Rabbi Hili offered the following eulogy:

"Certainly there is a mine for silver,
and a place where gold is refined.
Iron is taken out of the earth,
and copper smelted from the rock." (Job 28:1-2)—
These things can be replaced if they are lost.
But a sage who has died—
who can bring a replacement for him?—
"But where can wisdom be found;
where is insight's place?
No one can estimate its value;
it cannot be found in the land of the living." (Job 28:12-13)

Jerusalem Talmud,
Horayot 3:5

41. When a person is dying, . . .
he brings in his money and says to it,
"I have worked hard for you—
night and day—
please redeem me from this death and save me."
And the money replies,
"But haven't you heard—
'Wealth is of no avail on the day of wrath'?" (Proverbs 11:4)

Pirke DeRebbi Eliezer 34

42. Rabbi Yossi says:
Respect other people's money* as much as you do your own.

Sayings of the Fathers 2:17

*Or "possessions."

43. Rabba bar Rav Adda said in the name of Rav:
Whoever marries a woman for her money
will have worthless children.

Kiddushin 70a

44. Rabbi Chama bar Chanina and Rabbi Hoshaya were taking a tour of the
synagogues of Lod.
Rabbi Chama bar Chanina said to Rabbi Hoshaya:

How much money my ancestors spent here [by building these synagogues]!
He replied:
How many souls they drowned here!
Were there no people here who wanted to study Torah [and who were not
able to because there wasn't enough scholarship money available]?

Jerusalem Talmud,
Shekalim 5:4

45. Rabbi Abun made the gates for The Great School of Torah Study.
When Rabbi Mana came to visit,
Rabbi Abun said:

See what I have done!

Rabbi Mana replied:

"Israel forgot their Creator by building great buildings" (Hoshea 8:14)—
were there no people here who wanted to study Torah [and who were prevented
from doing so because there wasn't enough scholarship money available]?

Jerusalem Talmud
Shekalim 5:4

46. Artebon sent a priceless pearl to Our Holy Rabbi [Rabbi Yehuda the Prince], and said,

"Send me back something of equal worth."
Rabbi Yehuda sent him a Mezuzah.

Artebon responded,

"What is this all about?
I sent you something priceless,
and you send, in return, something worth only a single coin?"

Rabbi Yehuda replied,

"All that you and I own can't be compared to the value of this.
Not only that—
you sent me something I have to guard,
but I sent you something that,
even when you are asleep,* will protect you."

> *Jerusalem Talmud,*
> *Peah 1:1*

*Or: "when you die."

47. Rabbi Yochanan said in the name of Rabbi Shimon ben Yochai:

What is the meaning of the verse,
"For I, the Lord, love justice;
I hate robbery with offerings"? (Isaiah 61:8)
It is like a human king who,
passing through a customs-house,
said to his servants,
"Pay the taxes to the tax collectors."
They replied,
"But don't all the taxes belong to you anyway?"

He answered back,

"Every traveller will learn from my personal example,
and, as a result,
no one will evade the taxes."
So, too, with the Holy One, blessed be He, Who said—
"I, the Lord, . . . hate robbery with offerings"—
My children will learn from My personal example,
and will keep away from robbery.

> *Sukkah 30a*

POVERTY

48. When Rabbi Yehoshua ben Levi went to Rome,
he saw marble pillars covered with sheets,
so they wouldn't crack from the heat,
nor freeze from the cold.
He also saw a poor person,
with only a reed mat under him
and another one on his back
[to protect him from the elements].

Pesikta DeRav Kahana 9:1
Mandelbaum I:148

49. There is nothing harder in the world than poverty.
It is the hardest kind of suffering in the world.

Exodus Rabba 31:12

50. Poverty is like death.

Nedarim 7b

51. It was taught:

[Though they are alive,]
four kinds of people are like they were dead:
a poor person,
someone who has leprosy,
a blind person,
and someone who has no children.

Nedarim 64b

52. [Isaiah said to Israel in the name of God,]
"Poor, storm-tossed one!" (Isaiah 54:11)
Poor—in righteous people;
Poor—in words of Torah;
Poor—in Mitzvot and good deeds.

Pesikta DeRav Kahana 18:2
Mandelbaum I:294

MITZVOT

53. Rav Yehuda said in the name of Rav:

It is prohibited for a person to eat anything
until he feeds his animal,
because the verse first says,
"And I will provide grass in the fields for your animals"
    (Deuteronomy 11:15)
and *only afterwards* does it say,
"and you shall eat and be satisfied." (Deuteronomy 11:15)

Gittin 62a

54. Rav Yehuda said in the name of Rav:

Hospitality is more important even than encountering God's Intimate
    Presence.

Shabbat 127a

55. Rav Nachman bar Yitzchak said:

We do not make Mitzvot into bundles.*

Pesachim 102b

*Bunching them together, performing two or more at the same time.

56. Rabbi Elazar said:

People on a Mitzvah-mission will not be harmed,
neither on their way there,
nor on the way back.

Pesachim 8b

57. Rabbi Elazar said:

People on a Mitzvah-mission will not be harmed.
This principle, however, does not apply
where there is a greater-than-normal chance of injury.

Pesachim 8b

58. Rabbi Chanina said:

Someone who is commanded to do something,
and does it,
is greater than
someone who is not commanded to do something,
and does it.

Bava Kamma 38a

59. Rabbi Yochanan said:

"Among the dead—I am released" (Psalm 88:6)—
when a person dies, he is free from performing Mitzvot.

Shabbat 151b

60. Hillel used to say:

The more one eats,
the more one excretes.
The more fat one puts on,
the more food for the worms and maggots.
But the more good deeds,
the more well-being for the body.

Avot deRabbi Natan A:28

61. A stolen palm-branch [Lulav] . . . is unfit for Mitzvah-use.
A stolen myrtle-branch [Hadas] . . . is unfit for Mitzvah-use.
A stolen willow-branch [Arava] . . . is unfit for Mitzvah-use.
A stolen citron [Etrog] . . . is unfit for Mitzvah-use.

Mishna Sukkah 3:1, 2, 3, 5

62. Rabbi Abba said:

There are 248 positive Mitzvot in the Torah,
corresponding to the number of parts of the human body.
Each and every part of the body shouts to the person,
"Do a Mitzvah through me;
the benefit will be
that we will live,
and you will have a long life."
And there are 365 negative Mitzvot,
corresponding to the number of days in the solar year.
Every day, while the sun is shining, until it sets,
the sun shouts to the person,
"I decree through the authority of
the One Who has allowed the days to reach this day—
do not commit this transgression on me,
and don't weigh me and the whole world down
to the guilty side of the scale."
The sum is 613 Mitzvot.

Mechilta Ki Taytzay 2,
Buber, p. 33

63. It has been taught:
"This is My God, and I will glorify Him." (Exodus 15:2)—
Do the Mitzvot in His honor using beautiful Mitzvah-objects.
Make a beautiful Sukkah in His honor.
and a beautiful Lulav,
and a beautiful Shofar,
and beautiful Tzitzit,
and a beautiful Torah,
and write in it for its own sake in fine ink,
with a fine pen,
engaging an expert scribe,
and wrap it in beautiful silk.

Abba Shaul says:

"And I will glorify Him [ואנוהו]"
means "Be like Him"*—
just as He is gracious and compassionate,
so, too, should you be gracious and compassionate.

Shabbat 133b

*Abba Shaul explains ואנוהו to mean "I and He," playing on the similarity of the Hebrew to
the phrase אני והוא .

156

64. "Why should I fear in the time of trouble?—
It is because of the sins around my heels." (Psalm 49:6)

Blessed be the Name of the Holy One, blessed be He,
Who gave the Torah to Israel,
the Torah which has 613 Mitzvot in it,
some easy, some difficult.
And because there are easy ones
that people pay no attention to,
throwing them under their heels
(i.e., the easy ones),—
it is for that reason that David is afraid on the Day of Judgment,
saying,
"Master of the world,
I am not afraid of the difficult Mitzvot in the Torah—
they are difficult.
What am I afraid of?—
The easy Mitzvot.
Perhaps I transgressed one of them,
and I can't even remember if I did or not,
because it was so easy.
And You have clearly said,
'Be as careful of easy Mitzvot
as of the difficult ones.' "
It is for that reason that David said,
"Why should I fear in the time of trouble?—
It is because of the sins around my heels."

Tanchuma Ekev 1

157

SIMCHA-JOY

65. Rabbi Yitzchak bar Marion said:
The Torah teaches you a good rule of Menschlich living,
namely,
that when a person does a Mitzvah,
he should do it with a joyous heart.

Leviticus Rabba 34:8
Margoliot 4:790

66. "I therefore praised joy" (Ecclesiastes 8:15)—
This refers to the joy of doing Mitzvot.
". . . [I said] . . . of joy, 'What good is it?' " (Ecclesiastes 2:2)—
This refers to other, non-Mitzvah, kinds of joy.

Shabbat 30b

67. God's Holy Spirit infuses only hearts that are joyous.

Jerusalem Talmud,
Sukkah 5:1

68. Rabbi Ila said to Ulla:
When you get there [to Israel from Babylonia],
[show great respect] to my brother, Rav Beruna,
by greeting him in the presence of the entire assembly of sages,
because he is a great person,
and feels great joy when doing Mitzvot.
He once performed the Mitzvah of praying
[in an exceptional way],*
and did not stop smiling the entire day.

Berachot 9b

*Connecting the blessing of "Redemption" right before dawn, with the "Eighteen Blessings" right after dawn.

69. Rabbi Elazar said in the name of Rabbi Chanina:

. . . Two joyous occasions [Simchas] should not be mixed together.

Mo'ed Katan 8b

THE HEART

70. The Holy One, blessed be He, wants the heart.

Sanhedrin 106b

71. Rabbi Levi said:

. . . .

It is written,
"Give your heart to Me, my son;
Let your eyes watch My ways." (Proverbs 23:26)
The Holy One, blessed be He, said,
"If you give Me your heart and eyes,
I know you are Mine."

Jerusalem Talmud,
Berachot 1:5

72. Rava bar Mechasia said in the name of Rav Chama bar Goria
in the name of Rav: . . .
Any pain is better than pain in the heart.

Shabbat 11a

73. Rabbi Avdimi from Haifa said:

Before a person eats and drinks, he has two hearts,
but after he eats and drinks, he has only one.

Bava Batra 12b

TORAH II:
THE LIVES OF THE REBBIS

74. Rava said to Rafram bar Papa:
Please tell us some of the good things Rav Huna used to do.

He said to him:
I do not remember things from his youth,
but I do remember things from his old age. . . .
[One of the things he used to do was]—
whenever he was about to sit down and eat,
he would open his door and say,
"Whoever needs to, may come in and eat."

Ta'anit 20b

75. When Rabbi Chanina ben Tradyon was summoned
[after being arrested by the Romans,]
they asked:
Why did you continue to be involved in Torah-study
[even though you knew it was a capital offense]?

He replied:
I was simply doing what the Lord my God commanded me.

They immediately ruled
that he be burned to death,
that his wife be killed,
and that his daughter be placed in a whorehouse.

Avoda Zara 18a

76. Rabban Yochanan ben Zakkai had five students,
and he characterized each by the following phrases:

Rabbi Eliezer ben Hyrcanus
is a plastered cistern that never loses a drop;
a container covered with pitch that keeps in the wine.

Yehoshua ben Chanania
is a "three-stranded cord that is not easily broken." (Ecclesiastes 4:12)

Yossi HaKohen
is the saintly one of the generation.

Shimon ben Netan'el
is a desert oasis that holds onto its water.

Happy is the student whose teacher recognizes
his unique qualities
and publicly testifies to these talents!

And Elazar ben Arach
is a powerful stream
and a spring that keeps flowing with greater and greater force,
a personification of the verse,
"Your springs will gush forth
In streams in the public squares." (Proverbs 5:16)

Avot DeRabbi Natan A:14

77. Rabbi Yochanan ben Zakkai stepped out of the House of Torah-Study
[so that his student, Rabbi Eliezer, would not feel inhibited
when he was teaching.]
Rabbi Eliezer was sitting and expounding,
and his face was shining like the sun.
There were rays of light coming from him
like the rays of light Moses radiated
[when he received the Torah from God],
and no one could tell whether it was day or night.
Rabbi Yochanan ben Zakkai came up behind him
and kissed him on his head
and said to him,
"Happy are you,
Abraham, Isaac, and Jacob,
that this person is one of your descendants!"

Pirke DeRebbi Eliezer 2

78. It was said of Rabban Yochanan ben Zakkai that
   he never engaged in ordinary conversation,
   nor did he ever go four cubits without [studying] Torah,
   nor [four cubits] without Tfillin,
   nor did anyone ever get to the school of Torah-study before he did,
   nor did he ever sleep or nap in the school of Torah-study,
   nor did he think Torah-thoughts while in alleys where there was
      any filth,
   nor did he ever leave anyone behind in the school of Torah-study,*
   no one ever saw him sitting in silence, but rather always sitting
      and studying out loud,
   and no one ever opened a door for his students—he did it himself,
   and he never said anything [in Torah discussions] that he had not
      heard from his teacher,
   and he never said, "It is time to get up from Torah study"
      except on the eve of Passover and the eve of Yom Kippur.

As a result, his student, Rabbi Eliezer, acted in similar fashion.

Sukkah 28a

*He was the last one to leave.

RABBI AKIVA

79. Rabbi Akiva was Ben Kalba Savu'a's shepherd.
Ben Kalba Savu'a's daughter saw that Akiva had a genteel soul,
so she proposed to him, saying,
"If I let you marry me,
will you go study Torah?"
He said,
"Yes."

Ketubot 62b

80. Kalba Savua's daughter married Rabbi Akiva.
When Kalba Savu'a heard of it,
he disowned her.
They were married in the winter,
and they used to sleep on straw.
He used to pick straw out of his hair.
He said to her,
"If I only had the money,
I would buy you a Jerusalem of gold."
Elijah came to them in the form of a mortal
and called out at their gate,
"Give me some straw.
My wife is about to give birth,
and I have nothing for her to lie on."
Rabbi Akiva said to his wife,
"See—there is someone who doesn't even have straw!"

Nedarim 50a

81. Rabbi Akiva once made a City of Gold* for his wife.
Rabban Gamliel's wife saw it, became jealous,
and spoke to her husband about it.
He told her,
"Did you do for me
what she did for him?
She sold her hair and gave him the money
so that he would be able to study Torah."

Jerusalem Talmud,
Shabbat 6:1

*A "City of Gold" or "Jerusalem of Gold" was a piece of jewelry, a tiara with the shape of the city walls of Jerusalem cut into it.

82. What was the beginning of Rabbi Akiva's life of Torah study?
It was said that he was forty years old
and had not yet learned anything.
Once, while he was standing by a well,
he asked,
"Who cut a hole in this rock?"
They told him,
"The water that kept falling on it every day."
They also said,
"Akiva, don't you know the verse,
'Waters wear away even stones.'?" (Job 14:19)
Rabbi Akiva immediately began to reason about this
in the following manner:
If something so soft
can cut something so hard,
then, certainly, the words of Torah—
which are as hard as iron—
can engrave themselves on my heart,
which is only flesh and blood.

He and his son then went
to a teacher of little children.
He said,
"My teacher, teach me Torah!"
Rabbi Akiva held one end of the slate,
and his son the other.
The teacher wrote "Aleph, Bet" for him—
and he learned it,
"Aleph, Tav"—
and he learned it,
the Book of Leviticus—
and he learned it.
He just kept studying and studying
until he learned the entire Torah.

He then went and sat before Rabbi Eliezer and Rabbi Yehoshua.
He said to them,
"My teachers, open up for me
the meaning of the Oral Torah."
When they would tell him a specific law,
he would go and sit by himself and ask,
"This Aleph—why was it written?
This Bet—why was it written?
This thing—why was it said?"
He would then go back and ask them,
but they were dumbfounded by his questions.

Rabbi Shimon ben Elazar said,
"I will explain all of this [Akiva's Torah study]
by means of a parable:
There was a certain stonecutter
who used to cut stones in the mountains.
One day he took his pick-axe
and sat up on the mountain,
chipping away at the mountain pebble by pebble.
People came by and said to him,
'What are you doing?'
He replied,
'I am going to uproot this mountain
and toss it into the Jordan!'
They said,
'You can't uproot this whole mountain!'
But he kept cutting away and cutting away
until he came to a big boulder.
He crawled under it, loosened it,
uprooted it, and tossed it in the Jordan, proclaiming,
'This isn't your place—that is where you belong!'—
That's what Rabbi Akiva did to Rabbi Eliezer and Rabbi Yehoshua."

Rabbi Tarfon said,
"Akiva—there is a verse that refers to you:
He dams up the sources of the streams,
so that hidden things may be brought to light, (Job 28:11)—
things that used to be hidden from people,
you, Rabbi Akiva, have brought out into the light."

. . . .

Rabbi Akiva began to study Torah at age forty,
and thirteen years later he was teaching Torah
to crowds of people.

Avot DeRabbi Natan A:6

83. It was taught:
Rabbi Akiva said,
"When I was ignorant of Torah, I said,
'If I could get my hands on a sage,
I would bite him like a donkey!' "
His students said,
"Rebbi, say, 'Like a dog.' "
He said to them,
"There's a difference—
One [the donkey] bites and breaks bones,
the other [the dog] bites but doesn't break bones."

Pesachim 49b

84. It once happened that
Rabbi Akiva was sitting and teaching his students
when he remembered what he had done in his youth.

He said,

"I thank you, Lord, my God,
for making my portion among those
who sit in the school of Torah study,
and not among those
who hang around street corners."

Avot DeRabbi Natan A:21

85. Rabbi Akiva said:

If a person studied Torah in his youth,
he should also study Torah in his old age;
if he had students in his youth,
he should also have them in his old age.
A verse indicates this,
"Sow your seed in the morning,
[and do not hold back your hand in the evening,
since you do not know which is going to succeed,
the one or the other,
or if both are equally good.]" (Ecclesiastes 11:6)

Yevamot 62b

86. Rabbi Akiva once gave a banquet for his son.
    Whenever he opened a new barrel of wine he would say:
    To the lives of our teachers,
    and to the lives of their students!

Tosefta Shabbat 7 (8):9
Lieberman, p. 26

87. Whenever Rabbi Akiva would see Bar Kozeva,*
    he would say,
    "This is the King Messiah."

    Rabbi Yochanan ben Torata said to him,
    "Akiva, grass will grow from your cheeks
    before the Son of David will come."

Jerusalem Talmud,
Ta'anit 4:5

*i.e., Bar Kochba.

88. It once happened that
    Rabbi Eliezer, Rabbi Yehoshua, Rabbi Elazar ben Azaryah,
    Rabbi Akiva, and Rabbi Tarfon
    were reclining at the Passover Seder in B'nai B'rak.
    They spent the entire night
    speaking of the exodus from Egypt,
    until their students came and said,
    "Our teachers,
    it is time to recite the morning Shema."

Passover Haggadah

89. It was said that Rabbi Akiva had twelve thousand pairs of students
from G'vat to Antipatris,
and all of them died at the same period of time,
because they did not show appropriate respect for each other's dignity.
The world became desolate as a result,
until Rabbi Akiva came to the sages of the South
and [re-]taught them Torah.
[These sages were:]
Rabbi Meir, Rabbi Yehuda, Rabbi Yossi, Rabbi Shimon, and Rabbi Elazar
ben Shamu'a,
and they are the ones who brought the Torah back to life at that time.

One of the teachers taught:
They all died between Passover and Shavuot.

Rabbi Chama bar Abba,
and some say, Rabbi Chiyya bar Avin, said:
They all died a terrible death.
What was this terrible death?

Rabbi Nachman said:
Croup.

Yevamot 62b

90. Rabbi Akiva says:

. . . .

Whoever attaches himself to Mitzvah-doers—
even though he did not do as much as they did—
still receives a reward similar to theirs.

Avot de Rabbi Natan A:30

91. Rav Chelbo became sick,
so Rav Kahana went around announcing,
"Rav Chelbo is sick."
But no one came to visit him.
Rav Kahana then said [to the sages and students],
"Did it not once happen
that one of Rabbi Akiva's students became sick,
and none of the sages came to visit him?
So Rabbi Akiva went to visit,
and because they swept and washed the floor,
the student recovered.
Indeed, the student said,
'My teacher, you have given me new life!'
And right after that incident,
Rabbi Akiva went out and taught,
'Whoever does not perform the Mitzvah of visiting the sick—
it is as though he spilled someone's blood.' "

Nedarim 39b–40a

92. The Rabbis taught:
Rabbi Akiva instructed his son, Rabbi Yehoshua,
about seven things,
[One of them was]—
My son,
never go bursting into your own house,
[without knocking first]—
and so much more so,
never go bursting into another's house unannounced.

Pesachim 112a

93. Rabbi [Yehuda the Prince] used to show respect to the wealthy.
Rabbi Akiva used to show respect to the wealthy.

Eruvin 86a

94. Our rabbis taught:
Four went into the garden.
These are they—
Ben Azzai, and Ben Zoma, and The Other One [Elisha ben Abuya],
and Rabbi Akiva.

Rabbi Akiva said to them:
When you get to the pure marble pillars,
do not say, "Water, water,"
because a verse says,
"Whoever speaks untruths
shall not stand before my eyes." (Psalm 101:7)

Ben Azzai gazed and died. . . .
Ben Zoma gazed and went mad. . . .
The Other One hacked away at the plants.
Rabbi Akiva came out unharmed.

Chagiga 14b

95. When Rabbi Akiva's sons died,
all the Jews came and deeply lamented the loss.
When they were ready to leave,
Rabbi Akiva got up on a big bench and said,
"My brothers, the House of Israel, listen—
even though these two children were bridegrooms,
I am comforted because of the honor you have done.
And even though you might have done all this for Akiva—
see how many Akivas there are in the street!
[I suspect,] though, that this is what you said to yourselves,
'His God's Torah is in his heart.' (Psalm 37:31)
Because of that, so much the more is your reward—double.*
Now, go home to peace."

Mo'ed Katan 21b

*For the Mitzvot of comforting mourners and for honoring the Torah.

96. Torah study is not to be cancelled
when there is someone dying,
until he actually dies.

When Shimon, Rabbi Akiva's son, was sick,
Rabbi Akiva did not cancel Torah study,
but left messengers by his bedside.
The first one came and said,
"It is serious."
Rabbi Akiva said to the students,
"Continue to ask questions."
The second messenger came and said,
"His condition has taken a turn for the worse."
Rabbi Akiva returned the students to study.
The third one came and said,
"He is dying."
Rabbi Akiva said to the students,
"Continue to ask questions."
Then the fourth one came and said,
"He is at peace."
At that point, Rabbi Akiva stood up,
removed his Tfillin, tore his clothes,
and said to the students,
"My brothers, O Israel, listen:
Until now we were required to study Torah
Now I and you must do honor to the dead."

A great throng of people came in honor of Rabbi Akiva's son.
He said to them,
"Take a bench out for me from among the graves."
They took out a bench from among the graves,
and he sat down and taught,
"My brothers, O Israel, listen to me.
It is not that I am a sage—
there are people here who are greater sages than I am.
It is not that I am wealthy—
there are people here who are wealthier than I am.
People from the South know Rabbi Akiva,
but how would the Galileans know me?
The men know Rabbi Akiva,
but how would the women and children know me?
Yet I know your reward is great,
because the pain you have come with is for the sake of Torah
and the sake of the Mitzvah.

I am comforted—
even if I had had seven children
and had buried them along with my son.
It's not that a person wants to bury his children,
but I know that my son is privileged to be part of the Next World,
because he brought many people to do good,
and anyone who brings others to do good—
no sin can come through him. . . ."

Semachot 8:13,
Zlotnick p. 212–213

97. Rav Yehudah said in the name of Rav:
When Moses went up to Heaven [to receive the Torah],
he found the Holy One, blessed be He,
putting little crowns on the letters.
Moses said to Him,
"Master of the World, who is holding You back,
[that you have to add these touches to the Torah.
Isn't it good enough as it is?]"
He replied,
"There is a certain man who will appear
in a number of generations
named Akiva ben Yosef.
He will interpret from each of these little markings
hills upon hills of laws."
Moses said to him,
"Show him to me!"
God said,
"Turn around."
Moses went and sat
back in the eighth row [of Rabbi Akiva's school of Torah-study],
but he didn't understand a word of what was going on.
Moses began to feel uncomfortable,
until they got to a certain topic,
and one of the students asked,
"Our teacher, what is your source?"
To which Rabbi Akiva replied,
"It is a law handed down
from generation to generation—
all the way back to Moses from Sinai."
Then Moses relaxed.

He went back [to Heaven], and said to Him,
"Master of the World,
You have such an extraordinary person,
and yet You give the Torah through me?"
God replied,
"Be quiet.
This is the way I want things to be."

He said to Him,
"Master of the World,
You have shown me his Torah,
now show me his reward."
God said,
"Turn around."
He turned around and saw that
they were weighing out his flesh
in the meat market.
Moses said,
"Master of the World—
is this the reward for Torah?"
God replied,
"Be quiet.
This is the way I want things to be."

Menachot 29b

98. The Roman government once decreed destructive laws against the Jews,
dictating that they not study Torah.
Nevertheless, Rabbi Akiva and his colleagues studied Torah.*
Pappus ben Yehuda found him and said,
"You are endangering yourself by defying the law."
Rabbi Akiva replied,
"I will explain this all to you with a parable:
This situation is like a fox walking by a river.
He saw fish swimming around, looking for a place to hide.
The fox said to them,
'Come with me and I'll hide you in the rocks,
and then you won't have to be afraid.'
The fish replied,
'And you're the one everyone says is the smartest of all the animals?
You are really the stupidest.
Our whole lives are in the water,
and you tell us to come up to the dry land?

Look—if we are afraid in a place where we can live,
how much more so we'll be afraid where we will certainly die!'
So, too, with us [as Jews] —
Our whole lives are spent in Torah,
as it is written,
'It is your life and the length of your days' (Deuteronomy 30:20)—
and you are telling me,
'You are endangering yourself!"
Not long afterwards, both were arrested.
Pappus said to Rabbi Akiva,
"Happy are you that you were arrested because of Torah!
Woe to Pappus, who was arrested for worthless reasons!"
When they took Rabbi Akiva out to kill him,
it was the time for reciting the Shema.
Though they were raking his flesh with iron combs,
still, he was reciting the Shema.

Tanchuma, Ki Tavo 2

*In Berachot 61b the text states that he "taught Torah to crowds—openly." There are other
significant variations to the account of Rabbi Akiva's death on that page, and in the Jerusalem
Talmud, Berachot 9:5

99. When the news reached Rabbi Yehudah ben Betayrah and Rabbi Chanina
ben Tradyon
that Rabbi Akiva had been killed in Caesarea,
they put on sackcloth and said,
"Our brothers, O Israel, listen to us:
Rabbi Akiva was not killed
because he was suspected of robbery,
nor because he did not labor at Torah-study with all his might.
No, he was killed as a sign. . . .
In just a short while
there won't be any place in the Land of Israel
where there won't be bodies thrown everywhere. . . ."
It was said that
shortly thereafter the Roman armies came
and the whole world became chaotic. . . .
Within a year,
everything they predicted had come true.

Semachot 8:9
Zlotnick p. 214

HILLEL

100. Our Rabbis have taught:
One should always be as unassuming as Hillel,
and not as irascible as Shammai.

It once happened that two people made the following bet:
Whoever makes Hillel angry will win 400 *Zuz*.
One of them said,
"I will make Hillel angry."

It was Friday afternoon,
and Hillel was shampooing his hair.
The man went to Hillel's door and shouted,
"Anybody here named Hillel?
Anybody here named Hillel?"
Hillel put on a robe and went out to see him.
He said,
"My son, what is it that you want?"
The man replied,
"I have a question to ask."
Hillel said,
"Ask, my son, ask."
"Why do Babylonians* have such [unpleasantly] rounded heads?"
Hillel said to him,
"My son, you have asked a great question.
It is because their midwives are not very skilled."

The man went away and waited a while.
He then came back again and shouted,
"Anybody here named Hillel?
Anybody here named Hillel?"
Hillel put on a robe and went out to see him.
He said to him,
"My son, what is it that you want?"
He said to him,
"I have a question to ask."
Hillel said,
"Ask, my son, ask.
"Why do people from Palmyra have drippy eyes?"

*Hillel was a Babylonian by birth.

Hillel said to him,
"My son, you have asked a great question.
It is because they live in sandy places."

The man went away and waited a while.
He then came back again and shouted,
"Anybody here named Hillel?
Anybody here named Hillel?"
Hillel put on a robe and went out to see him.
He said to him,
"My son, what is it that you want?"
He said to him,
"I have a question to ask."
Hillel said,
"Ask, my son, ask."
"Why do Africans have such wide feet?"
Hillel said to him,
"My son, you have asked a great question.
It is because they live in swampy places."

The man said to Hillel,
"I have many questions to ask,
but I am afraid you will get angry."
Hillel wrapped his robe up well
and sat down before the man, saying,
"Any and all questions you might have to ask—ask them."
The man said,
"Are you the Hillel everyone calls 'Prince of Israel'?"
Hillel replied,
"Yes."
The man said,
"If you are he,
I hope there are not many more like you among the Jews!"
Hillel said,
"My son, why is that?"
He answered,
"Because I lost 400 *Zuz* because of you."
Hillel replied,
"Be careful with your emotions.
It is better that you lose 400 *Zuz*—
and even another 400—
than for Hillel to get angry."

Shabbat 30b–31a

176

TORAH III:
STUDY

101. Rabbi Chiyya bar Ammi said in the name of Ulla:
A person should always live
in the same place as his Master-Torah-Teacher [Rebbi].

Berachot 8a

102. What does the unwise person say?
"Who can learn the Torah?
Just the section *Nezikin* by itself is thirty chapters long!
Just the section *Kaylim* by itself is thirty chapters long!"

What does the wise person say?
"I will study two laws today
and another two tomorrow,
until I have learned the entire Torah."

Leviticus Rabba 19:2
Margoliot 2:417

103. Rav Acha bar Adda said in the name of Rav,
(and some say it was Rav Acha bar Abba said in the name of Rav Hamnuna
in the name of Rav):
Even the ordinary conversation of the sages needs to be studied.

Avoda Zara 19b

104. Rava said to the sages:
Please, don't come to study with me
at Nisan-time and Tishrei-time;*
otherwise you will have a difficult time providing for yourselves
all year.

Rabba Bar Bar Channa said in the name of Rabbi Yochanan in the name
of Rabbi Yehuda the son of Rabbi Ila'i:
Take note of the difference between
the earlier generations and the latter generations—
The earlier generations considered Torah primary,
and making a living was something they did on the side.
As a result, both endeavors succeeded.
The latter generations considered making a living primary,
and Torah-study only secondary.
As a result, neither endeavor succeeded.

Berachot 35b

*Nisan and Tishrei were seasons of harvest and other intense agricultural activity.

105. Rav Yehuda said:
Night was created for sleep.

Rabbi Shimon ben Lakish said:
Moonlight was created for [nighttime] Torah study.

Eruvin 65a

106. Our Rabbis have taught:
If a person was taken captive,
and so was his father and his Rebbi,*
he is to be redeemed before his Rebbi,
and his Rebbi before his father.
His mother takes precedence over all of them.

Horayot 13a

*"Rebbi" refers to his mentor, masterteacher, the one who taught, or teaches him the kind of
Torah that is most critical in his life.

107. Even a person who studies the Written Torah and the Oral Torah,
but does not apprentice himself to the sages,
is considered just a plain Jew [Am Ha'Aretz],
[and not a sage].

Sotah 22a

108. Rabbi Ila'i bar Yevarechya said:
If two sages live in the same city,
but do not relate decently to each other in Halachic matters
[—enough to learn from each other and teach each other—]
one will die,
and the other will go into exile.

Sotah 49a

109. Rava said:
Any sage who gets angry—
it is the Torah that is causing him to get worked up,
as the verse states,
"See, my word is like fire—declares the Lord." (Jeremiah 23:29)

And Rav Ashi said:
Any sage who is not as hard as iron
is not a sage,
as the verse states,
["See my word is like . . .]
a hammer that shatters rock." (Jeremiah 23:29)

Ravina said:
Nevertheless,
a person should train himself to be gentle,
as the verse states,
"Remove anger from your heart,
[and thereby dispose of a terrible human quality.]" (Ecclesiastes 11:10)

Ta'anit 4a

110. Rav Yehuda said in the name of Rav:
What is the meaning of this verse,
"Do not touch My anointed ones;*
do not harm My prophets"? (II Chronicles 16:22)
"Do not touch My anointed ones"*—
this refers to young children who are studying Torah;
"do not harm my prophets"—
this refers to students of the sages.

Shabbat 119b

*The Hebrew term, "Mashiach," may refer to kings and priests, who were anointed with oil when they assumed their positions of authority. Other interpreters understand the word to mean "Messiah."

111. When a person gets Torah-wisdom,
shrewdness comes along with it.

Sotah 21b

112. It was taught in the name of Rabbi Meir:
The serpent's ruin corresponded to its stature—
"the shrewdest of all" (Genesis 3:1),
"more cursed . . . than all." (Genesis 3:14)

Genesis Rabba 19:1

SHORT

113. You can always tell a squash by its stalk.

Berachot 48a

114. [Rav Ashi said to Ravina:]
Are we, then, mere cane-cutters in a bog?

Sanhedrin 33a

115. The saying goes:
Dance for me
for as much or as little money as I have.

Midrash on Psalms 16:13

116. It has been taught:
Rabbi Natan says—
Don't taunt someone else
with a shortcoming you yourself have.

Bava Metzia 59b

117. Rav said to Rav Asi:
Don't live in a place
where horses don't neigh
and dogs don't bark.
And don't live in a city
where the mayor is a doctor.
And don't marry two wives;
if you marry two—marry a third.

Pesachim 113a

118. Rav Pappa said:
No creature is poorer than a dog,
none richer than a pig.

Shabbat 155b

119. It is easy to acquire an enemy,
but it is difficult to acquire a friend.

Yalkut Shimoni,
VaEtchanan 845

120. [Choni the Circle Maker said:]
Without friends,
a person is better off dead.

Ta'anit 23a

121. If your friend calls you an ass,
put a saddle on your back.

If you have any shortcomings—
you be the first to reveal them.

Though the wine belongs to the host,
the butler gets the praise.

A hungry dog will eat even stones.

If you will help lift the load,
then I will lift also;
if not,
then I will not do it alone.

Bava Kamma 92b

122. The saying goes:
If there has been a hanging in someone's family,
don't say to him,
"Hang this fish up for me."

Bava Metzia 59b

123. Rabbi Yishmael taught:
"Choose life" (Deuteronomy 30:19)—
this refers to a craft or a trade.

Jerusalem Talmud,
Kiddushin 1:7

124. People are not held responsible for what they say when they are in pain and distress.

Bava Batra 16b

BLESSINGS AND PRAYERS

125. One who sees a friend after a thirty-day period
of being apart, recites the Shehecheyanu-blessing*;
after twelve months, he recites the blessing,
"[God,] Who brings the dead back to life."
These blessings apply only for very good friends,
and only if there is real joy in their reunion.

Shulchan Aruch,
Orach Chaim 225:1

*"Blessed are You, O Lord, our God, Ruler of the universe, Who has kept us alive and allowed
us to reach this occasion."

126. One who is outside in Nisan-time*
and sees trees just beginning to bloom,
recites the following blessing:
Blessed are You, O Lord our God,
Ruler of the Universe,
Who has made the world so full
it lacks nothing,
and has created in it
beautiful creations and beautiful trees
for human beings to enjoy.

Shulchan Aruch,
Orach Chaim 226:1

*Springtime.

127. One who sees 600,000 Jews together
recites the following blessing:
Blessed are You, O Lord, our God,
Ruler of the universe,
Wise One, Who knows everyone's innermost thoughts.

Shulchan Aruch,
Orach Chaim 224:5

128. One who sees a Jewish sage
recites the following blessing:
Blessed are You, O Lord, our God,
Ruler of the universe,
Who has imparted some of His wisdom
to those who stand in awe of Him.

One who sees a non-Jewish sage
who is distinguished for his secular wisdom
recites the following blessing:
Blessed are You, O Lord, our God,
Ruler of the universe, Who has given of His wisdom to human beings.

Shulchan Aruch,
Orach Chaim 224:6–7

129. Rav Zutra bar Tovia said in the name of Rav:
How do we know that there is a blessing for fragrances?
A verse states,
"The whole soul should praise God." (Psalm 150:6)—
And what kind of experience does the soul alone enjoy,
and not the body?—
One would think—fragrances.

Berachot 43b

130. It is prohibited to enjoy a pleasant fragrance
until a blessing is recited before smelling,
though afterwards there is no need to make a blessing.
If the object from which the fragrance is being emitted
is a tree or a part of a tree,
the blessing is,
"Who creates fragrant kinds of wood."
If it is a plant [or grassy substance],
the blessing is,
"Who creates fragrant plants."
If it is neither a tree nor a plant,
but rather something like musk,
the blessing is,
"Who creates many kinds of fragrances."
If it is a fruit that is edible,
the blessing is,
"Who gives fruits a lovely fragrance."

This last case applies
only when the fruit was selected to smell it
or to eat and smell,
but if it was selected just to eat,
and there was no intention to smell it—
even though it had a wonderful fragrance—
no blessing for the fragrance is recited.

Shulchan Aruch,
Orach Chaim 216:1-2

131. [When visiting the sick,]
the visitor should include this individual sick person
in prayers that also include other Jews who are ill,
saying:
May God be merciful unto you
and the other Jews who are ill.

Shulchan Aruch,
Yoreh De'ah 335:6

132. Rav Yehuda became ill and then recovered.
Rav Channa of Baghdad and the sages went to see him.
They said:
Blessed is the Merciful One
Who has given you back to us
and has not given you over to the dust.

Berachot 54b

133. Four categories of people
should express particular gratitude to God:
Those who have completed sea voyages;
those who have arrived at settlements
after passing through the desert;
those who have recovered from an illness, and
those who have been freed from prison. . . .

What is the blessing they recite?
Blessed are You, O Lord our God,
Ruler of the universe,
Who is gracious even to those who might not be worthy—
You have graciously extended great kindness to me.

Those who hear the recitation of this blessing
should respond:
May the One Who has graciously extended great kindness to you
continue to do so, Selah.

This blessing should be recited
in the presence of ten people. . . .
and it is customary to recite this blessing
after the reading of the Torah.

*Shulchan Aruch,
Orach Chaim 219:1-3*

134. In Rabbi Yannai's school of Torah-study it was taught:
Upon awakening in the morning, one should recite the following—
Blessed are You, O God, Who revives the dead.
My Master, I have sinned against You.
May it be Your will, God, my Lord,
that You give me
a good heart,
a good portion [in life],
an inclination to do good,
a good friend,
a good reputation
a good eye,*
and a good essence,
and a humble essence,
and a humble spirit.
May Your name not be desecrated through us,
and let us not become subjects of mockery
in the conversations of any other human beings,
and do not let our ultimate end be destruction,
nor our ultimate hope be despair.
And do not leave us so desperate as to need
the gifts of human beings,
who are only flesh and blood,
nor at the mercy of human beings,
who are only flesh and blood,
for our food—
for their gifts are minimal,
but the humiliation they inflict is great.
May our lives' lot be in Your Torah,
in the company of those who do Your will.

*i.e., a generous nature.

187

Rebuild Your house,
Your palatial Sanctum,
Your city,
and Your Temple.
Quickly.
In our days.

Jerusalem Talmud,
Berachot 4:2

CHILDREN

135. (*In the First Book of Samuel, Chapter I, the story of Channah, the Prophet Samuel's mother, is told. Before his birth, she was unable to bear children, and it is because of her impassioned prayer to God that she is granted a child. The Talmud has a lengthy passage discussing her prayer—its contents, its forthrightness, its specific requests. The following selection represents a number of rabbis' attempts to understand specifically what kind of child she wanted to have.*)

Rav said:
A prominent man.

Shmuel said:
A child who will anoint two kings, namely, Saul and David.

Rabbi Yochanan said:
A child equal to two people—Moses and Aaron. . . .

The Rabbis said: . . .
An average child.
When Rav Dimi came [from Palestine to Babylonia],
he explained this to mean:
Not too tall and not too short;
not too puny and not too bulky;
not too pale and not too reddish,
not exceptionally smart and not too slow-to-learn.

Berachot 31b

136. Our Rabbis taught:
A father has the following obligations towards his son—
to circumcise him,
to redeem him, if he is a firstborn,
to teach him Torah,
to find him a wife,
and to teach him a craft or a trade.
Some say he must also teach him how to swim.
Rabbi Yehuda says:
Whoever doesn't teach his son a craft or a trade
teaches him robbery.
Do we really think he teaches him robbery?

189

Rather, what we mean to say is:
it is as though he teaches him robbery.
. . . . and if his father did not have him circumcised,
the court is required to have him circumcised.
If the court does not do this,
then he, himself, later on, must have it done.
. . . . and if his father did not redeem him,
he is required to redeem himself.
. . . . and if his father did not teach him Torah,
he is required to teach himself.

Kiddushin 29a–b

137. It once happened that the son of Gorgios ran away from school.
His father threatened to hit him on the ears,
and he was so terrified by the threat,
he drowned himself in a cistern.
They consulted Rabbi Tarfon [concerning the funeral rites],
and he said:
No rites whatsoever are to be withheld.

Another incident happened with a young child from B'nai B'rak
who had broken a small bottle.
His father threatened to hit him on the ears,
and he went and drowned himself in a cistern.
They came and consulted Rabbi Akiva,
who said:
No rites whatsoever are to be withheld.

As a result of these incidents
the sages said:
A person should not threaten a child.
Rather—
he should spank him immediately
or keep his mouth shut and say nothing.

Semachot 2:4–5
Zlotnick p. 232

138. Rabbi Zera said:
One should not say to a child,
"I am going to give you something"
and then not give it to him,
because, as a result, he will be teaching him to lie,
as one verse puts it,
"They have trained their tongues to speak lies." (Jeremiah 9:4)

Sukkah 46b

139. The folk saying goes:
What the child says out in the street
comes either from his father or his mother.

Sukkah 56b

COMMUNITY LEADERSHIP

140. Rabbi Yehuda Nesi'ah and the Rabbis disagreed.

One said:
Accordingly to the leader, so the generation.

The other said:
According to the generation, so the leader.

Arachin 17a

141. When Rabbi Chaggai would appoint communal leaders,
he would teach them Torah,
explaining that all authority is given
by virtue of its Torah-source—
"Through me* kings reign . . .
Through me princes rule." (Proverbs 8:15–16)

Jerusalem Talmud,
Pe'ah 8:6

*i.e., the Torah.

142. There are four kinds of people no one can stand:
[One of them is]
a communal leader who is arrogant towards his constituents
for no good reason.

Pesachim 113b

143. Rabbi Chama bar Chanina said:
Why did Joseph die before his brothers?
Because he flaunted his authority.

Berachot 55a

THE SYNAGOGUE

144. We may sell a synagogue,
  and, similarly, all holy objects—
  even a Sefer Torah—
  in order to provide for Torah students,
  or to marry off orphans,
  with the money from the sales.

Shulchan Aruch,
Orach Chaim 153:6

145. There are those who prohibit entering a synagogue with a long knife.

Shulchan Aruch,
Orach Chaim 151:6

146. It is permitted to make a synagogue into a school of Torah study,
  but a school of Torah study may not be made into a synagogue.

Shulchan Aruch,
Orach Chaim 153:1

147. Members of a community may force each other to build a synagogue, and to
  buy a Torah, the Prophets, and the Writings.*

Shulchan Aruch,
Orach Chaim 150:1

*The three parts of the Bible.

148: The synagogue must be built on the high point of the city.
  It must be high enough so that it is higher than any other of the city's buildings that are in use. . .
  Gloss: In time of emergency, or when there is a fear of the government that
  would prevent them building a synagogue according to these rules, it
  is permissible to pray in a house, even though people live upstairs, as
  long as the people living upstairs keep their place clean.

Shulchan Aruch,
Orach Chaim 150:2,
With Isserles

149. If a person has made his house higher than the synagogue,
there are those who say he may be forced to lower it.

Shulchan Aruch,
Orach Chaim 150:3

150. *Gloss: The Bimah is to be placed in the center of the synagogue.*
This is where the Torah-reader stands, so that everyone may hear.
When the cantor [Sheliach Tzibbur] is praying, he should face
the Holy Ark.
The seating plan is as follows:
The Elders sit facing the people,
and the rest of the people sit in rows facing the Holy Ark
and the Elders.

Isserles to
Shulchan Aruch,
Orach Chaim 150:5

151. People should not act irreverently in synagogues nor in schools of
Torah study, as, for example:
[senseless] laughter, goofing around, and meaningless chatter.
People should not eat or drink in these buildings
nor overdress in them
nor simply stroll around in them,
nor come in just because of the heat or the rain.
Sages and their students may eat and drink in them
if it is absolutely necessary.
(Gloss: And some say they may eat and drink in the school
of Torah study even if there are no extraordinary circumstances.)
People may not conduct business in these buildings,
unless it is Mitzvah-business, for example:
budgeting Tzedakah funds and redeeming captives.
Eulogies may not be recited there
except for one of the distinguished members of the city
and for whom the entire community will come to share in the eulogizing.
If, however, a person has to come into these buildings
for purely personal reasons,
as, for example, to locate someone,
he should read over some written Torah-text
or recite some selection of Oral Torah
and then try to find the person,
so that it will not appear that he entered just for his own purposes.

And if he does not know how to study the Written or Oral Torah,
  he should say to one of the children,
  "Read me the verse you are studying,"
  or let him stay around for a while and then go,
  because the very act of sitting in these buildings is a Mitzvah,
  as it is written,
  "Happy are they who sit in Your house." (Psalm 84:5)

Shulchan Aruch,
Orach Chaim 151:1

152. A person may not sleep in a synagogue—not even a short nap—
  though this is permitted in a school of Torah study.

Shulchan Aruch,
Orach Chaim 151:3

153. If there is some synagogue-necessity involved,
  it is permitted to eat and sleep in the building.
  For this reason, people sleep in the synagogue on the night of
  Yom Kippur.
  And even if it is necessary for some other Mitzvah, . . .
  it is permitted to eat there.

Shulchan Aruch,
Orach Chaim 151:4

154. If a synagogue has two doors, a person may not go in one of them
  to make it a shortcut to get to and out the other door.

Shulchan Aruch,
Orach Chaim 151:5

155. It is considered proper to clean the mud off one's feet before
  coming in to pray.
  It is considered inappropriate for people to come to synagogue
  when one's clothes or body are dirty.

Shulchan Aruch,
Orach Chaim 151:8

156. The customary way to honor synagogues is to sweep and mop their floors.
It is also customary to light candles in them in order to show them
proper respect.

Shulchan Aruch,
Orach Chaim 151:9

157. A synagogue may not be torn down in order to build another,
because it may happen that,
due to circumstances beyond the congregation's control,
they will not succeed in building the other one.
Therefore, the new one should be built first,
and then the old one may be torn down. . . .
This applies to a situation where the first one was strong,
but if its foundations have rotted,
or its walls are tottering and about to cave in,
it must be torn down immediately,
and rebuilding must begin immediately,
quickly, day and night,
to prevent time and circumstance from causing insurmountable
difficulties leaving the building in a state of ruin.

Shulchan Aruch,
Orach Chaim 152:1

158. If a house was built just as a house,
and then afterwards it was dedicated as a synagogue,
it is considered a synagogue,
[and all the rules of a synagogue apply to it.]
However, it is not considered holy
until people have prayed in it.

Shulchan Aruch,
Orach Chaim 153:8

159. After leaving the synagogue,
> a person should go to the school of Torah study,
> and should establish a permanent time to study.

That time of Torah study should be so permanent
> that the person will not cancel it
> even if he thinks he will make a great financial profit.

Gloss: Even someone who does not know how to study
> *should go to the school of Torah study,*
> *as there is a reward for simply going there.*

Or he should set aside a place
> *and study a little of whatever he can manage to understand,*
> *and consider his position,**
> *and, thereby, a sense of the Awe of Heaven will enter his heart.*

> *Shulchan Aruch,*
> *Orach Chaim 155:1*
> *With Isserles*

*A prominent commentary, the Mishna Berura, understands "consider his position" to mean: While he is sitting, free of other responsibilities during this time in the school of Torah study, he should examine carefully if there might not be some aspect of wrongdoing in his business affairs: stealing, overcharging, too much interest, and the like, [and then decide] to stop doing those things.

160. Afterwards, a person should proceed to his business affairs,
> because any Torah study which is not linked to work
> will eventually come to nothing,
> and attracts sin to it,
> because poverty will cause him to transgress his Creator's wishes.

In any event, however,
> he should not make his work his primary occupation,
> but rather secondary, instead—
> his Torah study being primary.

As a result, both [the work and the Torah study] will succeed.
He should carry out his business affairs in good faith. . . .

> *Shulchan Aruch,*
> *Orach Chaim 156:1*

A MISCELLANY

161. Rabbi Alexandri once announced,
"Who wants life? Who wants life?
Everyone gathered around him and said,
"Give us life!"
He said to them,
" 'Who is the person who wants life,
who desires years of good fortune?
Guard your tongue from evil,
your lips from deceitful speech.
Shun evil and do good,
seek integrity and pursue it.' " (Psalm 34:13–15)

Avoda Zara 19b

162. It is a positive Mitzvah to remove any obstruction which is potentially lethal,
and to be careful of it, and to be extremely cautious about it, as the verse
states, "Be careful and watch yourself." (Deuteronomy 4:9)
And if anyone does not remove the obstacles that are potentially lethal, but
rather leaves them as they are, he has ignored a positive Mitzvah and has
transgressed the negative Mitzvah of "You shall not be the cause of bloodguilt
in your house." (Deuteronomy 22:8)

Maimonides, Mishnah Torah,
Laws of the Murderer and Self-Preservation 11:4

163. The sages have forbidden many things because they are potentially lethal,
and anyone who disregards them, saying,
"I'll go and endanger myself . . . . and what difference does it make to
anyone else anyway?"
or is not careful about these things—
[the court] may whip him for his defiance.

Maimonides, Mishnah Torah,
Laws of the Murderer and Self-Preservation 11:5

164. A woman who has recently given birth may wear shoes [on Yom Kippur], up to thirty days after giving birth.

A sick person also has a similar thirty-day period, even though it is not a dangerous illness.

So, too, [the thirty days' period] for one who has wounds on his feet.

Shulchan Aruch,
Orach Chaim 614:3

165. Anyone may wear shoes [on Yom Kippur] if there is danger of scorpions or similar dangerous creatures—
so that he should not be bitten if there are scorpions or other stinging creatures around.

Gloss: If it was raining, and the person wanted to go home from the synagogue or to the synagogue from home, and if he has a delicate constitution, he may wear shoes until he gets to where he is going.

Shulchan Aruch,
Orach Chaim 414:4
With Isserles

166. The Midrash-Interpreters* say:
Would you like to become acquainted with
The One Who spoke and, as a result, the world came into being?
Then study Midrash,
because when you study it
you will become acquainted with
The One Who spoke and, as a result, the world came into being,
and you will become attached to His ways.

Sifray Deuteronomy,
Ekev 49
Finkelstein, p. 115

*"Dorshay Haggadot." Here, as in other passages, "Midrash, "Haggadah," and "Aggadah" are essentially interchangeable.

167. [King David said:]
You [O God] know that—
even when I was living with complete peace of mind—
I did not forget You.

Midrash Psalms 139:2

168. Rabbi Eliezer said to his students:
My children,
do not trust in wealth,
nor in wisdom, nor in strength,
for a verse states,
"Thus says the Lord:
Let not the wise man glory in his wisdom;
Let not the strong man glory in his strength;
Let not the rich man glory in his riches.
But only in this should one glory:
In his earnest devotion to Me.
For I the Lord act with kindness,
Justice and equity in the world;
For in these I delight,
declares the Lord." (Jeremiah 9:22–23)

Tanna DeVay Eliahu Zuta 24
Ish-Shalom, part II:42

169. Rava bar Mechasia said
in the name of Rav Chama bar Guria
in the name of Rav:
A person should look around
to find a place to live
that was only recently founded,
because, since it was only recently settled,
it has fewer sins.

Shabbat 10b

170. Since the Tribe of Dan was the most populous
of all the tribes,
they marched last
[throughout the forty years' of wandering in the wilderness.]
They were responsible for returning any objects
anyone might have lost along the way.

Jerusalem Talmud,
Eruvin 5:1

171. Our Rabbis taught:
Forty-eight male prophets
and seven female prophets prophesied to Israel.
. . . .
It was taught:
Many prophets arose among Israel—
twice as many as the masses who left Egypt—
but only those prophecies that were needed for future generations were
written down,
and those that were not needed, were not recorded.

Megillah 14a

172. It was taught—
Rabbi Meir used to say:
Nobody should put pressure on another to eat with him
if he knows full well that he won't,
and nobody should send another many gifts
if he knows full well that he will not accept them.

Chullin 94a

173. In the Future Time,
the Holy One, blessed be He,
will take the corners of the Land of Israel,
and shake out all the uncleanness from it,
just like a person shakes out a piece of clothing,
slinging away everything that was on it.

Pirke DeRebbi Eliezer 34

201

DEATH

174. Nine Hundred and three kinds of death were created in the world.
. . . the easiest is the kiss [of God].

Berachot 8a

175. Rabbi Elazar HaKappar said:

. . . .

Without asking you,* you were formed, and
without asking you,   you were born, and
without asking you,   you live, and
without asking you,   you will die, and
without asking you,   you will give a final accounting
      in the presence of the King of Kings of Kings,
      the Holy One, blessed be He.

Sayings of the Fathers, 4:end

*or: "Against your will"; or "By God's decision."

176. It is prohibited for a mourner
to eat his own food
for the first meal after the funeral,
though it is permitted for the second meal,
even on the first day.
It is a Mitzvah for the neighbors
to prepare their own food for the mourner,
[for the first meal,]
so that he won't have to eat of his own food.

Shulchan Aruch,
Yoreh De'ah 378:1

177. There were two Ethiopians,
Elichoref and Achiya, the sons of Shisha, (I Kings 4:3)
who served King Solomon as scribes.
One day Solomon saw that the Angel of Death was sad.
He said to him:
Why are you sad?
He replied:
They [in Heaven] want me
to bring them two Ethiopians who live here.
Solomon put them in the custody of some demons,
who took them to the vicinity of Luz,
[where no one dies—
in an attempt to save their lives.]
When they got to the vicinity of Luz,
they died.
The next day Solomon saw the Angel of Death in a good mood.
He said to him:
Why are you in such a good mood?
He replied:
You sent them to the exact place
from which they [in Heaven] wanted me to take them.
At that point Solomon proclaimed:
A person's feet are responsible for him.
They will lead him to the place
where he is wanted.

Sukkah 53a

178. Shmuel said:
Anyone who wants to get a taste of death should put on shoes and
sleep in them.

Yoma 78b

GLOSSARY

Aleph: The first letter of the Hebrew alphabet. Other letters mentioned: Bet, Tav.

Bima: Pulpit or reader's stand in a synagogue.

Bracha: A blessing.

Havdalah: A ceremony at the end of the Sabbath composed of several blessings involving wine, spices, a candle—stressing the distinction between the Sabbath and the week-days.

Kiddush: The blessing over wine.

Menschlichkeit: The quality of being fully human; upright, decent, kind and caring. (Adj.: Menschlich)

Mezuzah: A small container with an inscription from the Torah hung on the doorposts of Jewish houses, according to instructions in Deuteronomy 6.

Mitzvah: Command, instruction, good deed done according to the prescriptions of traditional Jewish texts, such as visiting the sick, comforting morners, giving Tzedakah. (Plural: Mitzvot)

Rabbi: A person's essential teacher, master-teacher, primary source of Torah-wisdom and texts.

Sanhedrin: The Talmudic high court composed of distinguished sages.

Seder: Passover-night ritual of reciting the tale of the Exodus from Egypt.

Sefer Torah: A Torah-scroll.

Shabbat: The Sabbath.

Shema: "Hear O Israel," a text from Deuteronomy Chapter 6, recited morning and evening during regular prayers; a declaration of faith in God, which, later, in Jewish history, was recited by martyrs—since the First Century.

Shofar: Ram's horn, blown in synagogue on Rosh HaShana and Yom Kippur.

Sukkah: A flimsy boothlike structure where religious Jews live during the days of the Sukkot-festival.

Tfillin: A set of two leather straps with boxes attached, containing certain portions of the Torah, worn by religious Jews on their arm and forehead during morning prayers.

Torah: Literally "teaching"; originally meaning the Five Books of Moses, or Pentateuch; expanded to mean the entirety of Jewish study and learning.

Tosefta: A part of the early body of Talmudic literature, from the first two centuries of the Common Era.

Tzedakah: The distinctly Jewish method of performing charitable acts. From the Hebrew word "Tzedek," meaning "justice" or "what is right."

Tzitzit: The ritual fringes on the corners of a Tallis (prayer-shawl).

Yom Kippur: The Day of Repentance, holiest of the Holy Days, the entire day being spent in prayer, fasting, and repentance.

Zuz: An ancient coin.

Note: All references to Midrash Rabba are according to the Grossman Edition, "Hotza'at Midrash," New York, 1971.

TOPICAL INDEX TO
Where Heaven and Earth Touch

COMPILED BY BETH HUPPIN

Book One (I), Two (II) and Three (III)

DANNY SIEGEL, a 1993 recipient of the prestigious Covenant Award for Exceptional Jewish Educators, has been described by writer Leonard Fein as "American Jewry's leading expert in micro-philanthropy." As chairman of the Ziv Tzedakah Fund, which he founded 14 years ago, he has collected nearly $2 million for grass-roots community projects worldwide. He lectures to synagogues, Jewish Federations, religious schools, and university student groups about the dozens of mitzvah people he has met, and encourages his audiences to get involved...to fix the world...to make a difference.

Professor Gerald Bubis once referred to Danny Siegel as the "feeling person's thinker." When not on the road, Danny lives, works, and writes in Rockville, Maryland. He is the author of 20 books of prose and poetry, and has also written three books for children.